JAMESTOWN  EDUCATION

The Outer Edge™
Cool Science

Henry Billings
Melissa Billings

 Glencoe

New York, New York   Columbus, Ohio   Chicago, Illinois   Peoria, Illinois   Woodland Hills, California

Reviewers

Kati Pearson
Literacy Coordinator
Carver Middle School
4500 West Columbia Street
Orlando, FL 32811

Suzanne Zweig
Reading Specialist
Sullivan High School
6631 North Bosworth Avenue
Chicago, IL 60626

Beth Dalton
Reading Consultant
Los Angeles County Office
    of Education
9300 Imperial Avenue
Downey, CA 90240

Susan Jones
Reading Specialist
Alief Hastings High School
12301 High Star
Houston, Texas 77072

The McGraw-Hill Companies

Copyright © 2006 The McGraw-Hill Companies, Inc.
All rights reserved. Except as permitted under the United States Copyright Act, no
part of this publication may be reproduced or distributed in any form or by any
means, or stored in a database or retrieval system, without prior written permission
of the publisher.

ISBN: 0-07-869053-6

Send all queries to:
Glencoe/McGraw-Hill
8787 Orion Place
Columbus, OH 43240-4027

4 5 6 7 8 9 024 10 09 08 07

Contents

Unit Three

To the Student

Just about everybody is interested in how things work. When we want to know about what a robot can do, or how machines help us, or what scientists know about outer space, we can read about these things. There are 13 true stories in this book. In them you will learn about some interesting facts about science and how things work.

As you do the lessons in this book, you will improve your reading skills. This will help you increase your reading comprehension. You will also improve your thinking skills. The lessons include types of questions often found on state and national tests. Working with these questions will help you prepare for tests you may have to take in the future.

How to Use This Book

About the Book. *Cool Science* has three units. Each one has four lessons. Each lesson starts with a true story. The stories are about the ways that science has changed people's lives or may change lives in the future. Each story is followed by a group of seven exercises. They test comprehension and thinking skills. They will help you understand and think about what you read. At the end of the lesson, you can give your personal response. You can also rate how well you understood what you read.

The Sample Lesson The first lesson in the book is a sample. It explains how to complete the questions. It also shows how to score your answers. The correct answers are printed in lighter type. In some cases, the reasons an answer is correct are given. Studying these reasons will help you learn how to think through the questions. You might have questions about how to do the exercises or score them. If so, you should ask those questions now, before you start Unit One.

Working Through Each Lesson. Start each lesson by looking at the photo. Next read the caption. Before you read the story, guess what you think it will be about. Then read the story.

After you finish the story, do the exercises. Study the directions for each exercise. They will tell you how to mark your answers. Do all seven exercises. Then check your work. Your teacher will give you an answer key to do this. Follow the directions after each exercise to find your score. At the end of the lesson, add up your total score. Record that score on the graph on page 115.

At the end of each unit, you will complete a Compare and Contrast Chart. The chart will help you see what some of the stories in that unit have in common. It will also help you explore your own ideas about the events in the stories.

Sample Lesson

Seeing for the First Time

As you read this, someone in the world is going blind. It happens every five seconds. There are 45 million blind people in the world. That may sound sad. But what is really sad is that most of them don't need to be blind.

2   It seems that doctors can do miracles with eyes. Often they can give people back their sight. Or they can keep someone from going blind in the first place. But some countries don't have good eye care. That is true of Bangladesh. It is a poor country in Asia. It has 140 million people. But it has just 600 eye doctors. So most people there don't get help for their eye problems.

3   When they do get help, their lives can be changed. Harun-ur-Rashid knows all about that. He was born blind. So were his five children. But thanks to doctors, they can now see.

4   Harun was born with cataracts. That means the lenses on the inside of his eyes were cloudy. Often, cataracts come with age. But some people are born with cloudy lenses. The lenses of Harun's eyes were so cloudy that he was blind from the day he was born.

5   As a child, Harun lived a sad life. He could not go to school. He could not work. By the time he was nine, he was begging on the streets. Then one day, something wonderful happened. A stranger took him to an eye hospital. Doctors there did a small operation. They made a tiny cut in each eye. That let them get to the cloudy lenses. The doctors took these out. Then they put in new, clear lenses. It was a bit like putting in new windows to take the place of dirty ones. When the doctors were done, Harun could see. In the United States, doctors do this work all the time. But Harun had never dreamed of such a thing. He could hardly believe it.

6   "I never saw the face of the man who helped me, who picked me off the street, took me to the hospital, and changed my life," said Harun. If he ever did meet the man, Harun said, he would give him a hug. He would let the man know how much his sight meant to him.

7   Harun grew up and got married. But his troubles were not over. He and his wife had five children. All of these children were born with cataracts. None of them could see a thing.

Shown here is Harun-ur-Rashid with two of his children. Harun and his five children were blind until doctors operated on their eyes.

8 Harun did not know what to do. There were no eye doctors in his village. Besides, he had no money. His job was to take people places. He pulled them around in a cart. He worked 12 hours a day, seven days a week. Still, he only made two dollars a day. That was barely enough to buy beans and rice for his family.

9 Harun took the children to the wisest people in his village. They tried to help. "But nothing worked," Harun said. Because the children were blind, they could not go to school. They stayed in their one-room hut. They had no friends and very little hope.

10 Then, in 2002, Harun got lucky again. Once more, strangers changed his life. This time the strangers came from the Childhood Blindness Project. This group began in England. It sent workers to Bangladesh. The workers looked for blind people who could be helped by doctors.

11 The workers heard about Harun. They got in touch with him. They told him they could help his children. Then they made plans with an eye hospital in the city of Dhaka. And so one day, Harun and his five children left their home. They made the six-hour trip to the eye hospital. It was not easy. The children held hands to help each other along. In Dhaka, doctors were ready. They took out the cataracts in each child's eyes.

12 The operations went well. Each one took just half an hour. And each one cost about $60. That may not seem like much money. But it was more than Harun would ever have. Luckily, the Childhood Blindness Project took care of the bill.

13 Harun was filled with joy. "I was so happy when I saw that my children could see," he said.

14 His children felt the same way. Nine days later, Harun brought them home. For the first time in their lives, they saw what their village looked like. When they saw their mother, Mariam, tears fell from their eyes.

15 "I just feel so happy that I can see the faces of my father and mother, my brothers and sisters," said one of the boys.

16 His brother put it this way. He said that before the operation, he could not play. He could only sit in his house. "All I knew is that I could not see anything and I was unhappy. Before, it was a world of darkness, and now there is light."

A Finding the Main Idea

One statement below tells the main idea of the article. One statement is too general, or too broad. The other statement explains only part of the article; it is too narrow. Label the statements using the following key:

M—Main Idea   B—Too Broad   N—Too Narrow

___B___ 1. Being able to see is very important. People all over the world have eye problems and cannot see. Giving them the gift of sight can change their lives. [This statement is true, but it is *too broad.* It does not tell anything about Harun-ur-Rashid and his children.]

___M___ 2. Harun-ur-Rashid, born with cataracts, was given the gift of sight by a stranger who took him to an eye doctor. Others made sure that Harun's children got operations too. [This statement is the *main idea.* It tells you that the article is about Harun-ur-Rashid and his children and how they were given the gift of sight.]

___N___ 3. Harun-ur-Rashid had five children who had cataracts. Because they could not see, they stayed at home all the time. [This statement is true, but it is *too narrow.* It gives only a few facts from the article.]

Score 4 points for each correct answer.

_____ **Total Score:** Finding the Main Idea

B Recalling Facts

How well do you remember the facts in the article? Put an X in the box next to the answer that correctly completes each statement.

1. Harun-ur-Rashid lives in

☐ a. England.
☒ b. Bangladesh.
☐ c. the United States.

2. To help Harun see, the doctors

☒ a. did an operation.
☐ b. put drops in his eyes.
☐ c. gave him some pills.

3. Harun's children were helped by the

☐ a. same stranger who had helped their father.
☐ b. United States.
☒ c. Childhood Blindness Project.

4. Nine days after their eye operations, the children

☐ a. went to England.
☒ b. went back home.
☐ c. had operations on their feet.

Score 4 points for each correct answer.

_____ **Total Score:** Recalling Facts

C | Making Inferences

When you draw a conclusion that is not directly stated in the text, you are making an inference. Put an X in the box next to the statement that is a correct inference.

1.

☒ a. Without help from outside the family, Harun and his children would still be blind.

☐ b. If Harun had worked harder, he could have saved up enough money for the eye operations for his children.

☐ c. Doctors who did the operations on the children didn't ask anyone to pay for it.

2.

☐ a. It seems that Harun has been angry most of his life because he and his children were born blind.

☒ b. Each eye doctor in Bangladesh must take care of many people.

☐ c. It takes a very long time to see after you have a cataract operation.

Score 4 points for each correct answer.

_____ **Total Score:** Making Inferences

D | Using Words

Put an X in the box next to the definition below that is closest in meaning to the underlined word.

1. Kittens are <u>blind</u> until they are about a week old. Then they open their eyes and can see everything.

☐ a. not able to make noises

☐ b. not able to hear

☒ c. not able to see

2. When the dog was found, after being lost for six months, we all started believing in <u>miracles</u>.

☐ a. terrible things

☒ b. wonderful things

☐ c. funny things

3. About a <u>million</u> people live in that big city.

☒ a. 1,000,000

☐ b. 1,000

☐ c. 100

4. Because George had <u>cataracts</u>, he could not read books. Someone had to read them aloud to him.

☐ a. blue eyes

☐ b. clear eyes

☒ c. cloudy eyes

5. Doctors put new <u>lenses</u> into Kelly's eyes to help her see more clearly.

- ☐ a. the hair around the eyes
- ☐ b. the watery parts of eyes
- ☒ c. the clear parts of eyes

6. A few weeks after the doctor did the <u>operation</u> on Mr. Brown's heart, he felt much better.

- ☐ a. a pill given to sick people to make them feel better
- ☒ b. set of actions done to fix a problem with the body
- ☐ c. a get-well card sent to a sick person

Score 4 points for each correct answer.

_____ **Total Score:** Using Words

E | Author's Approach

Put an X in the box next to the correct answer.

1. The main purpose of the first paragraph is to

- ☐ a. tell how many people there are in the world.
- ☒ b. say that people are going blind all the time.
- ☐ c. make the reader afraid of going blind.

2. From the statements below, choose the one that you believe the author would agree with.

- ☐ a. Harun's life would probably not have been much different if he had stayed blind.
- ☐ b. For people with eye problems, Bangladesh would be a good place to live.
- ☒ c. People who help other people see are doing a good thing.

3. The author probably wrote this article in order to

- ☒ a. tell how strangers helped Harun and his family see.
- ☐ b. teach readers how to care for their eyes.
- ☐ c. show how different eye care in Bangladesh is from eye care in the United States.

Score 4 points for each correct answer.

_____ **Total Score:** Author's Approach

F	**Summarizing and Paraphrasing**

Put an X in the box next to the correct answer.

1. Which summary says all the important things?

☐ a. Harun-ur-Rashid lives in Bangladesh, a poor country in Asia. Harun had been born with cataracts. His five children were born with cataracts too. [This summary misses too many important details.]

☐ b. The Childhood Blindness Project looks for blind people who can be helped by doctors. This group started in England. They do good work in places such as Bangladesh, a poor country in Asia. [This summary misses too many important details.]

☒ c. Harun-ur-Rashid was born blind. A stranger took him to a hospital where the doctors operated on him to help him see. Years later, the Childhood Blindness Project gave cataract operations to his children. [This summary says all the most important things.]

2. Which sentence means the same thing as the following sentence? "But Harun had never dreamed of such a thing."

☐ a. But Harun had never been able to sleep well at night.

☒ b. But Harun had never thought about this. [If someone "had never dreamed of such a thing," it means that he or she had never thought about it.]

☐ c. But Harun never had any dreams when he slept.

> Score 4 points for each correct answer.
>
> _____ **Total Score:** Summarizing and Paraphrasing

G	**Critical Thinking**

Put an X in the box next to the correct answer.

1. Choose the statement below that states an opinion.

☒ a. Everyone should send money to the Childhood Blindness Project.

☐ b. There are about 140 million people in Bangladesh.

☐ c. Harun's job was to pull people around in a cart.

2. Harun and his wife, Mariam, are different because

☐ a. only Mariam lived in Bangladesh.

☒ b. only Harun was born blind.

☐ c. only Mariam went with the children to get their operations.

3. What was the cause of Harun's eye problems?

☐ a. His eyes had been hurt in an operation.

☐ b. He had hurt his eyes in a car crash.

☒ c. He had been born with cataracts.

4. In which paragraph did you find your information or details to answer question 3?

☐ a. paragraph 1

☒ b. paragraph 4

☐ c. paragraph 6

5. How are the eye operations that Harun and his children had an example of cool science?

☒ a. Using science, doctors were able to help Harun and his family see.

☐ b. The eye operations cost so much that Harun couldn't pay for them himself.

☐ c. The eye operations were paid for by the Childhood Blindness Project in England.

Score 4 points for each correct answer.

_____ **Total Score:** Critical Thinking

Enter your score for each activity. Add the scores together. Record your total score on the graph on page 115.

_____ Finding the Main Idea

_____ Recalling Facts

_____ Making Inferences

_____ Using Words

_____ Author's Approach

_____ Summarizing and Paraphrasing

_____ Critical Thinking

_____ **Total Score**

Personal Response

Describe a time when you or someone you know got help from a stranger. [In a few words, tell about a time in your life when a stranger helped you, someone else in your family, or a friend. It could have been something big or something little.]

_____

_____

_____

Self-Assessment

I can't really understand how _____

_____

_____

[Did you find anything puzzling about this article? Write about it here.]

Self-Assessment

You can take charge of your own progress. Here are some features to help you focus on your progress in learning reading and thinking skills.

Personal Response and Self-Assessment. These questions help you connect the stories to your life. They help you think about your understanding of what you have read.

Comprehension and Critical Thinking Progress Graph. A graph at the end of the book helps you to keep track of your progress. Check the graph often with your teacher. Together, decide whether you need more work on some skills. What types of skills cause you trouble? Talk with your teacher about ways to work on these.

A sample Progress Graph is shown on the right. The first three lessons have been filled in to show you how to use the graph.

Comprehension and Critical Thinking Progress Graph

Directions: Write your score for each lesson in the box under the number of the lesson. Then put a small X on the line directly above the number of the lesson and across from the score you earned. Chart your progress by drawing a line to connect the Xs.

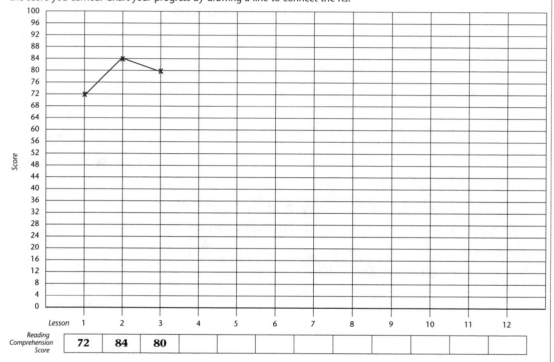

Lesson	1	2	3	4	5	6	7	8	9	10	11	12
Reading Comprehension Score	72	84	80									

UNIT ONE

Secret Lives of Animals

Listen carefully. Do you hear a rat laughing?

2   No, this isn't a joke. Researcher Jaak Panksepp spent months listening to the sounds that rats make. Believe it or not, he says they really do laugh.

3   Panksepp tested rats by tickling them. He tickled hundreds of them. Each time he did so, the rats made chirps and whistles. Panksepp says this is how rats laugh. The sounds are too high for people to hear. But using special tools, Panksepp could hear them. "It sounded like a playground," he said. In fact, he found that rats made the same noises when they rolled around and played with each other.

4   "We do think they have a sense of joy," Panksepp says.

5   A few years ago, no one would have believed this. But every year, researchers learn new things about animals. They have learned that some cats are right-handed. Others are left-handed. Crickets may chirp on cool days. But they chirp faster on hot days. Hippos can talk to each other on land. But they can also talk underwater.

6   Researchers often have a question in mind. For example, why do birds sing? We know they do it to send messages to other birds. But do they ever sing just for fun? Researchers spent years trying to find out. They now say the answer is yes. Some birds do seem to sing just for the joy of hearing their own voices.

7   Some researchers are surprised by what they find. Angela Ridgel is one of them. Ridgel worked with cockroaches. She knew they could walk up walls. She wanted to know how they did it. Ridgel found something strange. She found that old cockroaches move slower than young ones. They have trouble bending their legs. No one had known that growing old was hard on cockroaches. Now researchers are looking at old age in cockroaches. Ridgel's find could help people. This information could help scientists learn more about aging.

8   Joyce Poole did not have a question in mind. She just tried to learn all she could about elephants. For 25 years, Poole observed these animals. She saw them act happy. When friends met, for example, they all made loud roars. They flapped their ears wildly. They even danced around in circles. Poole says "elephants feel a deep sense of joy" when they see their old friends.

Scientists think some animals are very smart. Shown here is Rico, a Border collie dog. He is able to understand about 200 words of human language.

Poole also saw elephants grow sad. When one died, others stood next to it. They reached out with their trunks and touched it. Later, they carried its bones far away. Then they covered the bones with dirt.

9   Poole's work helped show that animals can have emotions. Other work has shown how smart they can be. Dr. Julia Fischer worked with a dog named Rico. This dog knows more than 200 words. Fischer put out toys for Rico. She asked him to bring certain ones to her. Rico brought the right toy 37 times out of 40. He even knew the name of a toy after hearing it just once. Fischer says that's as good as a three-year-old child could do.

10   Dolphins are smart animals too. In one test, researchers showed dolphins lots of different things. Then they put some of these things in the dolphins' pool. They asked the dolphins what was in there.

11   "Is there a ball?"

12   "Is there a hoop?"

13   The dolphins pushed on buttons to answer "yes" or "no." They almost always gave the right answer. They remembered the names of the things. And they could tell if these things were in their pool.

14   Researchers have found out something else about dolphins. They only let a half of their brain sleep at a time. One half always has to be awake. That's because dolphins must think in order to take a breath. So first they close their right eye. They shut down the left side of their brain. Then, after a while, they change sides. Dolphins will do this for eight hours a day. While one side of its brain naps, a dolphin does not move much. It just swims slowly near the top of the water. But it is awake enough to take breaths.

15   There are still lots of things we don't know about animals. And not all researchers agree on what has been learned so far. Some don't think rats really do laugh. Some don't think birds sing for fun. Indeed, it is not always easy to know what animals are doing. Chimps sometimes make a face that looks like a smile. But it turns out that this is how they show fear. So researchers have to be careful. Animals have many secrets. We will never learn them all. But the ones we do learn can help us understand our world a little better.

A | Finding the Main Idea

One statement below tells the main idea of the article. One statement is too general, or too broad. The other statement explains only part of the article; it is too narrow. Label the statements using the following key:

M—Main Idea   B—Too Broad   N—Too Narrow

_____ 1. It is important that we keep learning about the world in which we live. Researchers are helping us do that.

_____ 2. The work of some researchers tells us that animals feel and think more than we thought they did.

_____ 3. It seems that elephants care about each other. When one dies, the others touch it with their trunks and then cover its bones with dirt.

Score 4 points for each correct answer.

_____ **Total Score:** Finding the Main Idea

B | Recalling Facts

How well do you remember the facts in the article? Put an X in the box next to the answer that correctly completes each statement.

1. Researcher Jaak Panksepp says that when rats laugh, they

☐ a. make a clicking sound.
☐ b. scream loudly.
☐ c. chirp and whistle.

2. Angela Ridgel was surprised to find out that cockroaches

☐ a. are able to walk up walls.
☐ b. move slower when they get old.
☐ c. chirp when they are happy.

3. Dr. Julia Fischer says that a dog named Rico

☐ a. understands about 200 words.
☐ b. can walk up walls.
☐ c. can say about 200 words.

4. A dolphin sleeps

☐ a. all day.
☐ b. with half of its brain awake.
☐ c. with both eyes wide open.

Score 4 points for each correct answer.

_____ **Total Score:** Recalling Facts

C | Making Inferences

When you draw a conclusion that is not directly stated in the text, you are making an inference. Put an X in the box next to the statement that is a correct inference.

1.

☐ a. Jaak Panksepp thinks that rats like to be tickled.

☐ b. A researcher never does the same thing over and over.

☐ c. The only way to hear a rat laugh is to stand very close to it.

2.

☐ a. If you hear a bird sing, you can be sure that it is happy.

☐ b. In a race, a young cockroach would probably beat an old cockroach.

☐ c. Joyce Poole gets tired of things quickly.

Score 4 points for each correct answer.

_____ **Total Score:** Making Inferences

D | Using Words

Put an X in the box next to the definition below that is closest in meaning to the underlined word.

1. The <u>researcher</u> ran the tests over and over again until she was sure that her idea was right.

☐ a. someone who makes up stories

☐ b. someone who looks for new facts

☐ c. someone who is the head of a town or city

2. It is hard to kill <u>cockroaches</u> in your kitchen even if you step right on them.

☐ a. bugs with flat black bodies

☐ b. furry animals, like squirrels

☐ c. animals that live in the water

3. Vicki got a lot of <u>information</u> about the car she wanted before she bought it.

☐ a. money needed to buy things

☐ b. facts that can be known

☐ c. lies; ideas that are not true

4. Looking through the window of the classroom, the parents <u>observed </u>their children.

☐ a. hugged

☐ b. forgot

☐ c. watched

5. Some people hide their <u>emotions</u> and never let anyone see them cry.

☐ a. money

☐ b. friends

☐ c. feelings

6. You need to use your <u>brain</u> to know the answer to this riddle.

☐ a. the part of the body that takes in food

☐ b. the part of the body that thinks

☐ c. the part of the body that takes in air

Score 4 points for each correct answer.

_____ **Total Score:** Using Words

E | Author's Approach

Put an X in the box next to the correct answer.

1. What is the author's purpose in writing this article?

☐ a. to show that we can learn a lot about animals

☐ b. to tell the reader about the way dolphins sleep

☐ c. to describe what happens when elephants die

2. From the statements below, choose the one that you believe the author would agree with.

☐ a. All researchers agree that rats laugh because they are happy.

☐ b. Elephants are nicer than dogs or dolphins.

☐ c. It is a good idea to learn more about animals.

3. The author tells this story mainly by

☐ a. telling about what happened to the researchers and the animals in time order.

☐ b. looking at different animals and telling what is known about them.

☐ c. making up stories about what might have happened to people and animals.

Score 4 points for each correct answer.

_____ **Total Score:** Author's Approach

F | Summarizing and Paraphrasing

Put an X in the box next to the correct answer.

1. Which summary says all the important things about the article?

☐ a. After looking carefully at animals such as rats, insects, birds, and elephants, some researchers say that animals have feelings. Other researchers have learned that animals such as dogs and dolphins are smart.

☐ b. Most researchers agree that birds sing to send messages to other birds. But some researchers say that birds also sing just for the joy of hearing their own voices.

☐ c. One animal researcher says that dolphins can learn the names of things. When they were asked if certain things were in their pool, a group of dolphins almost always gave the right answer.

2. Which sentence means the same thing as the following sentence? "Rico brought the right toy 37 times out of 40."

☐ a. Rico hardly ever brought the right toy.

☐ b. Most times, Rico brought the right toy.

☐ c. No one knew whether Rico would bring the right toy.

Score 4 points for each correct answer.

_____ **Total Score:** Summarizing and Paraphrasing

G | Critical Thinking

Put an X in the box next to the correct answer.

1. Choose the statement below that states a fact.

☐ a. Joyce Poole watched elephants for 25 years and tried to learn more about them.

☐ b. No one with any sense would believe that rats laugh.

☐ c. Researchers use their time well when they spend it looking at animals.

2. From information in the article, you can predict that

☐ a. researchers will soon agree that rats laugh because they are happy.

☐ b. researchers will keep on looking at and testing animals.

☐ c. in a short time, people will know everything there is to know about animals.

3. The dog named Rico and dolphins are alike because

☐ a. they sleep with only one side of the brain.

☐ b. they recognize some words.

☐ c. they look like they are smiling when they are afraid.

4. In which paragraphs did you find the information or details to answer question 3?

☐ a. paragraphs 7 and 8

☐ b. paragraphs 8 and 9

☐ c. paragraphs 10 and 13

5. According to Joyce Poole, what is the cause of elephants' dancing in circles when they meet other elephants they know?

☐ a. The elephants feel afraid.

☐ b. The elephants feel angry.

☐ c. The elephants feel happy.

Score 4 points for each correct answer.

_____ **Total Score:** Critical Thinking

Enter your score for each activity. Add the scores together. Record your total score on the graph on page 115.

_____ Finding the Main Idea

_____ Recalling Facts

_____ Making Inferences

_____ Using Words

_____ Author's Approach

_____ Summarizing and Paraphrasing

_____ Critical Thinking

_____ **Total Score**

Personal Response

I agree with the author because _____

_____

Self-Assessment

While reading the article, _____ was the easiest for me.

The Robot That Eats Cars

Jim Potts had an idea. It was a wild idea—a really wild one. But the more Potts thought about it, the more he liked it. Near the end of 1987, Potts met with his friend Doug Malewicki. Malewicki loved to build new things. Potts thought Malewicki was just the person to make his idea come to life.

2   Potts's idea came from looking at children's toys. The toys are called Transformers. They can be changed from one thing to another. At first they look like toy trucks. But when parts of them are lifted, they change shape. They turn into toy robots.

3   "Hey, Doug," said Potts, "why don't you build a real Transformer? You know, a huge robot."

4   Malewicki loved the idea. It would be hard, but he thought he could do it. He decided to build a great Transformer. He wanted to make it so big it could eat cars. "Kids would love that," said Potts.

5   "Yes, yes, yes," said Malewicki. "People will love it."

6   Malewicki went right to work. He built a small copy of the Transformer out of wood. That helped him see whether his plans would work. They did. So then he built the real thing. It took Malewicki and his workers eight months to build it. It cost $2.5 million. Malewicki tested it for months. He fixed anything that didn't work right. At last, he was ready to show the world his new toy. He called it Robosaurus.

7   Malewicki took Robosaurus all over the country. He took it to Canada. He went to car shows and airplane shows. Huge numbers of people came. They all wanted to see Robosaurus. At each show, the lights were turned down. A truck came in. Its horn was going and its lights were flashing. Then it stopped. Suddenly, huge legs kicked out from the truck. The truck was changing shape. It was just like a Transformer. In seconds, the truck turned into Robosaurus!

8   People had never seen anything like Robosaurus. It looks a lot like a dinosaur. It stands 40 feet high. That's as tall as a four-story building. It is very heavy too. It is about 58,000 pounds. But that is not the best part. Robosaurus has long, sharp teeth. It has a strong mouth. Fire shoots out of its nose. Its hands can crush a car. Robosaurus even makes sounds like someone eating a big meal. It roars loudly. It also burps.

9   It takes a lot of gas to make Robosaurus move. In fact, it takes 300 gallons for the robot to go one mile.

The giant car-eating Transformer called Robosaurus is shown here during one of its performances.

So most of the time it stays folded up. It can be pulled by trucks from show to show.

10   As Potts and Malewicki had hoped, people loved Robosaurus. Everyone wanted to see it tear things apart. So at each show, Robosaurus is fed an old car. It picks up the car with its mouth. It pulls off the roof with its teeth. It bites the car in half. Its hands crush the car. Then it tosses the car to the ground. Finally, it burns the car with fire. The fire is so strong that it turns the car bright red. People in the front rows can feel just how hot it is.

11   Cars are not the only things Robosaurus can eat. Once in a while, it is fed a small plane. It has eaten trucks. Robosaurus has even eaten a house! It began by pulling off the roof. Then it burned the rest of the building down with a shot of fire.

12   It did not take long for Robosaurus to become a star. It was given parts in two movies. One was called *Wakin' Up in Reno.* The other was *The Recycler.* Robosaurus has been on TV many times. It was even the star of its own TV special.

13   Robosaurus is fun to watch. But it is hard to drive. It takes a long time to learn how to do it. The driver sits in a seat in Robosaurus's head. There are 18 different parts of the robot that can move. Some must be moved at the same time. Certain buttons move the robot's hands. Others move its head. And still others make the robot walk or turn. The driver uses his or her hands, fingers, arms, and feet to push these buttons. Next to the driver sits a second person. He or she also has jobs to do. One is to take care of the fire that shoots out of the robot's nose. Another is to turn on all the roars and burps that Robosaurus makes.

14   Reporters sometimes get to sit inside Robosaurus's head. José Diaz-Balart did this. Diaz-Balart is a TV reporter. He got the chance to drive Robosaurus. He made the robot pick up a car and crush it. Later, he told people what it had been like to drive Robosaurus.

15   "Let me tell you, it's a power rush," he said. "It'll bring out the mad scientist in anybody."

A | Finding the Main Idea

One statement below tells the main idea of the article. One statement is too general, or too broad. The other statement explains only part of the article; it is too narrow. Label the statements using the following key:

M—Main Idea   B—Too Broad   N—Too Narrow

_____ 1. Robosaurus, a huge robot, was hard to make. It took eight months to build it. It cost about $2.5 million. After Robosaurus was built, its maker tested it for months.

_____ 2. Not everyone can have a dream come true. But that is what happened to one man when he and a friend made the Robosaurus.

_____ 3. Doug Malewicki planned and made a huge robot that can eat big things such as cars. Robosaurus has appeared in movies. It has been all over the country. People love it.

Score 4 points for each correct answer.

_____ **Total Score:** Finding the Main Idea

B | Recalling Facts

How well do you remember the facts in the article? Put an X in the box next to the answer that correctly completes each statement.

1. Jim Potts brought his idea for a huge robot to his friend Doug Malewicki in

☐ a. 1958.
☐ b. 1987.
☐ c. 2003.

2. The idea for Robosaurus came from children's toys called

☐ a. Transformers.
☐ b. Shape Changers.
☐ c. Rocking Robots.

3. When Robosaurus starts its act, it looks like a big

☐ a. tiger.
☐ b. clown.
☐ c. truck.

4. Fire comes out Robosaurus's

☐ a. mouth.
☐ b. eyes.
☐ c. nose.

Score 4 points for each correct answer.

_____ **Total Score:** Recalling Facts

C | Making Inferences

When you draw a conclusion that is not directly stated in the text, you are making an inference. Put an X in the box next to the statement that is a correct inference.

1.

- [ ] a. Even before they made the robot, Jim and Doug were sure they would make a lot of money with it.
- [ ] b. Jim and Doug are people who like to do new and different things.
- [ ] c. Most people are too afraid of Robosaurus to like its act.

2.

- [ ] a. It would not cost much money to drive Robosaurus from show to show.
- [ ] b. Anyone who can drive a car would be able to drive Robosaurus.
- [ ] c. It would be a good idea to sit far away from Robosaurus when it burns a car or house.

Score 4 points for each correct answer.

_____ **Total Score:** Making Inferences

D | Using Words

Put an X in the box next to the definition below that is closest in meaning to the underlined word or phrase.

1. The tiny <u>robots</u> hummed as they zoomed around the kitchen floor mopping up the puddles.

- [ ] a. machines that look like people and do simple jobs
- [ ] b. people who clean houses
- [ ] c. stuffed toy animals

2. We believe that this <u>dinosaur</u> ate only green plants.

- [ ] a. a large body of fresh water
- [ ] b. a machine that digs in the ground
- [ ] c. an animal that lived long ago

3. After my uncle finishes eating, he sometimes <u>burps</u> out loud.

- [ ] a. licks one's lips and smiles
- [ ] b. lets air out of the stomach through the mouth
- [ ] c. pats one's stomach and smiles

4. Mom bought two <u>gallons</u> of milk at the food store.

- [ ] a. the money it takes to buy something
- [ ] b. large, heavy blocks
- [ ] c. a way of measuring liquids such as water

5. The <u>reporters</u> told fans that the team had a new player.

☐ a. people who plan large buildings

☐ b. people who tells jokes for pay

☐ c. people who gather and spread the news

6. After I won the two-mile race, I felt a <u>power rush</u> and decided to try a five-mile race.

☐ a. the idea that things are not working well

☐ b. a feeling that one can do anything

☐ c. a feeling of being very tired

Score 4 points for each correct answer.

_____ **Total Score:** Using Words

E │ Author's Approach

Put an X in the box next to the correct answer.

1. The author uses the first sentence of the article to

☐ a. tell why Jim Potts thought that Doug Malewicki could help him make the Robosaurus.

☐ b. tell the reader that Jim Potts came up with the idea of Robosaurus.

☐ c. show the difference between Jim Potts and Doug Malewicki.

2. Choose the statement below that best describes the author's opinion in paragraph 13.

☐ a. No one likes driving Robosaurus.

☐ b. Robosaurus has too many parts.

☐ c. Working Robosaurus is hard.

3. The author probably wrote this article in order to

☐ a. prove that people use too much money and time on things that are silly.

☐ b. show that people can do wonderful things if they try.

☐ c. stop people from going to see the Robosaurus.

Score 4 points for each correct answer.

_____ **Total Score:** Author's Approach

F Summarizing and Paraphrasing

Put an X in the box next to the correct answer.

1. Which summary says all the important things about the article?

☐ a. Jim Potts thought of Robosaurus, but he couldn't make it himself. He went to his friend Doug Malewicki. Malewicki thought it was a good idea and went to work on it right away. Everywhere Robosaurus is shown, people like seeing it.

☐ b. Robosaurus weighs about 58,000 pounds and is as tall as a four-story building. It has long teeth and a strong mouth for tearing things apart. It sounds like it is having a big meal when it eats cars.

☐ c. Robosaurus is a robot big enough to eat cars. It changes from a truck into a robot. Jim Potts came up with the idea, and Doug Malewicki planned and made it. People love to see it tear things apart and burn things in movies, on TV, and in shows.

2. Which sentence means the same thing as the following sentence? "Everyone wanted to see it tear things apart."

☐ a. Everybody wanted to watch it be torn into pieces.
☐ b. Everybody hoped to see it pull things apart.
☐ c. Everybody saw things pull it apart.

Score 4 points for each correct answer.

_____ **Total Score:** Summarizing and Paraphrasing

G Critical Thinking

Put an X in the box next to the correct answer.

1. Choose the statement below that states an opinion.

☐ a. Robosaurus is about 40 feet high.
☐ b. Robosaurus has been in two movies so far.
☐ c. Making Robosaurus was a great idea.

2. From information in the article, you can predict that

☐ a. Malewicki will soon take Robosaurus home and never show it to anyone else again.

☐ b. as long as people want to see Robosaurus, Malewicki will show it to them.

☐ c. Malewicki will soon take Robosaurus apart because no one wants to see it anymore.

3. A Transformer and Robosaurus are alike because

☐ a. they are toys that children own and play with.
☐ b. they eat cars, trucks, and houses.
☐ c. they change from one thing to another thing.

4. What is the effect of Robosaurus's using 300 gallons of gas to travel one mile?

☐ a. Robosaurus is pulled from show to show.
☐ b. Robosaurus has been in two movies.
☐ c. Robosaurus has 18 different moving parts.

5. How is Robosaurus an example of cool science?

☐ a. It took eight months to build Robosaurus.

☐ b. Scientists make robots. Robosaurus is a great robot.

☐ c. Robosaurus cost about $2.5 million to make.

Score 4 points for each correct answer.

_____ **Total Score:** Critical Thinking

Enter your score for each activity. Add the scores together. Record your total score on the graph on page 115.

_____ Finding the Main Idea

_____ Recalling Facts

_____ Making Inferences

_____ Using Words

_____ Author's Approach

_____ Summarizing and Paraphrasing

_____ Critical Thinking

_____ **Total Score**

Personal Response

A question I would like Doug Malewicki to answer is

" _____

_____?"

Self-Assessment

One of the things I did best when reading this article was

_____

I believe I did this well because

_____

A Gun That Saves Lives

It was 4 P.M. when police got the call. A man in Fresno, California, had just fired a gun at his neighbors. No one was hurt. But now the man was getting into his truck with the gun still in his hand. The police had to stop him. They chased him for a block. Then his truck hit two parked cars. He ran back to his house before police could stop him. The police ordered him to give up. He wouldn't.

2   For the next hour and a half, the police waited. At last the man came out. The police sent two dogs after him. But the man began hitting the dogs. Someone ran to help the dogs. But the man struck this person too. At last, police pulled out a new kind of gun and fired it at the man. He dropped to the ground. He was not dead. He was not even badly hurt. But for a few seconds, he could not move. The police ran in, grabbed him, and took him away.

3   This new kind of gun is a Taser gun. It does not shoot bullets. Instead, it gives out an electric charge.

Shown here is a Taser gun that some police use. It has an electric charge. A normal hit from the Taser lasts for five seconds.

The gun can be fired from up to 21 feet away. It sends out a dart tied to a wire. The dart sticks to a person's clothes. An electric charge is sent through the wire. The charge is so strong that it can go through thick clothes. One charge might last up to five seconds. Most of the time that is enough. It will knock a person off his or her feet. The police can then take the person away without trouble.

4   What does it feel like to be hit with a Taser? Len Ramirez, a TV news reporter, wanted to find out. He let a police officer shoot him. Ramirez got just a one-second charge. "It was bad," Ramirez wrote. He said that the shock ran through his legs and arms and made him fall off his chair. Luckily, he said, it was over quickly. Then he felt okay again.

5   For police officer Greg Stewart, the shock was longer. No one meant to "Tase" him. But it happened. The charge lasted five full seconds. Stewart said it felt like his eyes were popping out of his head. "The charge traveled down my neck, through my chest," he said. It hurt a lot. To him, five seconds "seemed like forever." His neck hurt so much that he missed two days of work.

6   Still, being Tased is better than being shot. That's how Phoenix police officer Tony Morales sees it. Suppose a man tries to hit an officer with a baseball bat.

In the past, Morales says, the man "was probably going to be shot." Now he might be Tased. That will stop him. But it might not cost him his life.

7 Phoenix police got Tasers in 2003. That cut in half their need to fire real guns. In Seattle there was more good news. In 2003 police there killed no one with guns. The same was true in Miami. There were no police shootings at all in Miami in 2003.

8 Not all people like Taser guns. For one thing, Tasers can hurt people. A few people have died after being hit by one. The shock is strong. It can be too much for a person's body. And there is one more problem. Some people say the police use Tasers too freely. Police did Tase one man seven times in a row. They Tased someone else after his hands were tied. A 71-year-old man was Tased. So was a nine-year-old girl. Richard Brown works with police in Portland, Oregon. He worries that "these things are being pulled out too quickly."

9 The case of Jose Jiminez Jr. shows both sides of the Taser question. In 2003 Jiminez was in Orlando, Florida. He was driving his car. Suddenly, the police pulled him over. They thought he was a robber. He wasn't. He just had the same kind of car as the robber. Jiminez did not like being stopped. He tried to brush the officer's hand off his arm. The officer thought Jiminez was reaching for a gun. So the officer pulled out his Taser and used it on Jiminez.

10 On the one hand, the Taser may have saved Jiminez's life. If the police had shot him with a gun, he might be dead. On the other hand, the officer might not have been so quick to shoot a real gun. So in that sense, maybe the Taser has hurt more than it has helped.

11 People who are in trouble with the police do not like Tasers. In fact, they have grown to fear them. In Phoenix the police trapped a robber. They took out their guns. The robber knew they wouldn't shoot. So he just laughed at them. Then another officer came. This one pulled out a Taser. The robber quickly put up his hands. He begged the officer not to Tase him.

12 "Bad guys like to talk to other bad guys," said one officer. "The word is out on the street."

A | Finding the Main Idea

One statement below tells the main idea of the article. One statement is too general, or too broad. The other statement explains only part of the article; it is too narrow. Label the statements using the following key:

M—Main Idea   B—Too Broad   N—Too Narrow

_____ 1. Police have a new tool. The Taser gun sends a shock that stops people from moving. Like other guns, Tasers can hurt people badly, so police must use them carefully.

_____ 2. Police in Seattle, who sometimes use Tasers, didn't kill anyone with real guns or Tasers in 2003. In Miami, where the police also use Tasers, there were no police shootings at all in 2003.

_____ 3. A new kind of gun is being used by police. Some people think that using it is a better idea than using a real gun. Other people feel that it brings about new problems for police.

Score 4 points for each correct answer.

_____ **Total Score:** Finding the Main Idea

B | Recalling Facts

How well do you remember the facts in the article? Put an X in the box next to the answer that correctly completes each statement.

1. Taser guns shoot out

☐ a. a stream of water.
☐ b. small bullets.
☐ c. an electric charge.

2. Most times, people hit by a Taser gun

☐ a. cannot move for a while.
☐ b. will never move again.
☐ c. die very quickly.

3. Some people worry that if the police have Taser guns, the officers

☐ a. will shoot too quickly.
☐ b. will be less safe.
☐ c. will forget how to use their real guns.

4. Jose Jiminez Jr. had been stopped by police in Orlando, Florida. He was Tased when he

☐ a. reached for his gun.
☐ b. tried to brush away the officer's hand.
☐ c. shot a police officer with a real gun.

Score 4 points for each correct answer.

_____ **Total Score:** Recalling Facts

C | Making Inferences

When you draw a conclusion that is not directly stated in the text, you are making an inference. Put an X in the box next to the statement that is a correct inference.

1.

☐ a. Police would rather not kill people, even if the people are doing something wrong.

☐ b. When police fire a Taser, they know that they won't kill anyone.

☐ c. No one saw a need for something like the Taser gun before a few years ago.

2.

☐ a. Soldiers who fight enemies who are far away from them should be given Tasers.

☐ b. The police don't keep track of how many people they shoot every year.

☐ c. The charge from a Taser gun does different things to different people.

Score 4 points for each correct answer.

_____ **Total Score:** Making Inferences

D | Using Words

Put an X in the box next to the definition below that is closest in meaning to the underlined word or phrase.

1. A falling branch <u>struck</u> Sharese on the head and knocked her to the ground.

☐ a. missed

☐ b. hit

☐ c. passed

2. Jay shot at the cans at the far side of the yard. His <u>bullets</u> knocked them off the fence.

☐ a. guns that can fire many times in a row

☐ b. knives thrown at something

☐ c. small balls shot from guns

3. If you touch a bare live wire, an <u>electric charge</u> will hurt you.

☐ a. a bright light

☐ b. a rush of power

☐ c. a loud sound

4. Stand back when she throws the <u>dart</u>, or it might stick into you.

☐ a. a short, sharp arrow

☐ b. a soft ball

☐ c. a round stone

5. The man was surprised when he felt the <u>shock</u> from the Taser gun run through his body.

☐ a. a warm, happy feeling

☐ b. a slow-spreading cold

☐ c. a sudden upsetting feeling

6. Omar asked Brad and his sister, "What do you <u>guys</u> want to do today?"

☐ a. people

☐ b. ghosts

☐ c. girls

Score 4 points for each correct answer.

_____ **Total Score:** Using Words

E | Author's Approach

Put an X in the box next to the correct answer.

1. The main purpose of the first paragraph is to

☐ a. tell how the Taser gun works.

☐ b. tell why the Taser gun is so important for police.

☐ c. tell about a problem the Fresno police were facing.

2. Choose the statement below that is the weakest argument for using a Taser gun.

☐ a. It gives police a chance to catch people without killing them.

☐ b. Some people can die after being hit with a Taser gun.

☐ c. Most times, it is safer to be shot by a Taser than by a real gun.

3. Choose the statement below that best explains how the author deals with the opposite point of view.

☐ a. The author says that writer Len Ramirez got Tased once. Ramirez said that it hurt him quite a lot.

☐ b. The author says that police in many cities believe that using Tasers has cut down on their shootings.

☐ c. The author says that although some people like Tasers, others fear that police might use them too much.

Score 4 points for each correct answer.

_____ **Total Score:** Author's Approach

F Summarizing and Paraphrasing

Put an X in the box next to the correct answer.

1. Which summary says all the important things about the article?

☐ a. After a man in Fresno, California, fired a gun at his neighbors, he went back into his house. Police waited for a long time for him to come out. Then he came out and started hitting dogs and a man. That is when police shot him with a Taser gun.

☐ b. The Taser gun can work from up to 21 feet away. The gun stops people from moving by giving out an electric charge. The charge may last only a few seconds. But it can knock a person off his or her feet.

☐ c. Taser guns are new guns that send out a charge. If you get shot by a Taser, you can't move. Many police believe that Tasers are good because most times these guns stop people without killing them. Police have to be careful that they don't use Tasers too much.

2. Which sentence means the same thing as the following sentence? "The word is out on the street."

☐ a. The news is spreading.

☐ b. The streets are filled with people.

☐ c. No one on the street talks anymore.

Score 4 points for each correct answer.

_____ **Total Score:** Summarizing and Paraphrasing

G Critical Thinking

Put an X in the box next to the correct answer.

1. Choose the statement below that states an opinion.

☐ a. Police should use only Tasers from now on.

☐ b. Being shot by a Taser can kill some people.

☐ c. Police in Phoenix got Tasers in 2003.

2. From information in the article, you can predict that

☐ a. Taser guns will soon be sold as children's toys.

☐ b. more police will begin using Taser guns.

☐ c. police will soon stop using Taser guns.

3. Taser guns and real guns are different because

☐ a. police use Taser guns, but they never use real guns.

☐ b. Tasers cannot kill people. Only real guns can kill people.

☐ c. Tasers shoot electric charges and real guns shoot bullets.

4. The police in Phoenix had trapped a robber. One officer pulled out a Taser. What was the effect of the officer's action?

☐ a. The robber quickly put up his hands.

☐ b. The robber laughed at the police.

☐ c. The robber gave back the money he had taken.

5. In which paragraph did you find the information or details to answer question 4?

☐ a. paragraph 6

☐ b. paragraph 7

☐ c. paragraph 11

Score 4 points for each correct answer.

_____ **Total Score:** Critical Thinking

Enter your score for each activity. Add the scores together. Record your total score on the graph on page 115.

_____ Finding the Main Idea

_____ Recalling Facts

_____ Making Inferences

_____ Using Words

_____ Author's Approach

_____ Summarizing and Paraphrasing

_____ Critical Thinking

_____ **Total Score**

Personal Response

Would you tell other students to read this article? Explain.

_____

_____

Self-Assessment

A word or phrase in the article that I do not understand is

_____

_____

A Helping Hand

Debbie Graham loved to swim. But one day in 1995, the 23-year-old teacher made a dive into a pool. She went too far. She hit her head on the other side. "I was face down in the water and could not move," she said. A friend quickly called for help. Debbie was rushed to the hospital. There her doctors gave her the bad news. She had broken her neck. Debbie was paralyzed. She would never again move her arms or legs.

2 The same kind of thing happened to Todd Anderson. In 1998 Todd was driving his truck to work. His wheels hit ice. The truck slid off the road. There was a big drop. The truck rolled over four or five times. Todd lived through the crash, but he was paralyzed from the chest down.

3 Thirteen-year-old Nichole Good hoped to join her school swim team. That dream ended one day in 1989. It was raining. Nichole's mother was driving her to a baby-sitting job. Suddenly, they saw a car. It was coming down the wrong side of the road! Her mother turned to get out of the way, but their car hit a tree. Nichole's mother wasn't hurt. But like Debbie and Todd, Nichole ended up paralyzed.

4 Debbie, Todd, and Nichole all faced a hard new life. They could not walk. They could not move their arms or hands. They could not even hold a glass of water. "I was unable to do anything for myself," said Debbie.

5 Losing the use of their legs was bad. But losing the use of their arms and hands was even worse. Debbie could think of lots of things she might still do without legs. But, she said, "There is not a lot you can do without your arms."

6 Still, there was some hope. Scientists were working on a new way to help paralyzed people. The idea was to get their hands to work again. After all, Debbie, Todd, and Nichole did still have hands. But messages from their brains could no longer get to these hands. So the hands were of no use. They could not hold things. They could not pick things up. They could not move at all.

7 Scientists hope to change that someday. They hope to repair paralyzed bodies. Then messages could once more get through. Until then, though, scientists needed a different plan. They had to find a new way to get messages to the hands.

Eric Schremp gives a thumbs-up sign. He was paralyzed in an accident. The Freehand System allowed him to move his hands again.

8   They came up with something called the Freehand System. It is a tiny box with lots of wires. This box does what the brain can no longer do. It sends messages to the hands. Doctors would cut into a paralyzed person's shoulder. Here they would place the box. Then they would run wires from the box down to the fingers. These wires would not show. They would be inside the arm. By moving the shoulder, a person could send a message to the box. The message would then travel down the wires to the hands. Moving the shoulder forward would send a message to open the hand. Moving the shoulder back would make the hand close.

9   Debbie, Todd, and Nichole could still move their shoulders. They wanted to try the box. So they each had an operation. They each had the box put in their shoulder.

10   The Freehand System worked beautifully. The first time Todd used it, he was able to reach for a glass of water. "I picked it up and was able to drink out of it," he said. The doctors were very happy. They could not believe how well he did.

11   Debbie cried when she first moved her hand. She hadn't moved it for six years. "Just to be able to reach out and pick something up has made me so much more independent," she said.

12   Nichole, too, felt as if she had been given a new life. "I'm able to eat and drink," she said. "I can brush my teeth. I'm much more independent now."

13   This was good news. There was some bad news too. The plan would not work for everyone. A person has to be able to move his or her shoulder. Also, the Freehand System is not easy to set up. Just putting the box and wires in place takes eight hours. Then there is a long wait. The cuts from the operation need to heal. So Debbie spent three weeks lying in bed. She spent two more months getting stronger. Only then did the doctors let her use her hand.

14   There is one other problem. The Freehand System costs a lot of money. Todd got his in 2001. He was the fifth and last person to get one at his hospital. No more are being made. People like Todd can still get help with ones they have. But no new ones are being sold.

15   Someday the costs might come down. Then more people will be able to drink a glass of water on their own. Debbie Graham, Todd Anderson, and Nichole Good know how great that can be.

A | Finding the Main Idea

One statement below tells the main idea of the article. One statement is too general, or too broad. The other statement explains only part of the article; it is too narrow. Label the statements using the following key:

M—Main Idea   **B—Too Broad**   **N—Too Narrow**

_____ 1. Todd Anderson lost the use of his arms and legs when he crashed his truck. Nichole Good was paralyzed when the car she was in hit a tree.

_____ 2. One good thing about science is that it can sometimes make people's lives better. People who can't move their hands have been helped by a wonderful new idea.

_____ 3. Scientists have come up with a way to help people who can't move their arms and hands. The Freehand System sends messages from the shoulders to the hands to make the hands move.

Score 4 points for each correct answer.

_____ **Total Score:** Finding the Main Idea

B | Recalling Facts

How well do you remember the facts in the article? Put an X in the box next to the answer that correctly completes each statement.

1. Debbie Graham broke her neck when

☐ a. she dove into a pool.
☐ b. her truck rolled over.
☐ c. her car hit a tree.

2. Nichole Good couldn't hold things because

☐ a. she no longer had hands to hold things.
☐ b. she could not move her shoulders forward and back.
☐ c. messages from her brain didn't reach her hands.

3. Doctors put the Freehand System boxes in

☐ a. Debbie's, Todd's, and Nichole's hands.
☐ b. Debbie's, Todd's, and Nichole's shoulders.
☐ c. Debbie's, Todd's, and Nichole's brains.

4. For the Freehand System to work, a person must be able to move his or her

☐ a. mouth.
☐ b. head.
☐ c. shoulders.

Score 4 points for each correct answer.

_____ **Total Score:** Recalling Facts

C | Making Inferences

When you draw a conclusion that is not directly stated in the text, you are making an inference. Put an X in the box next to the statement that is a correct inference.

1.

☐ a. People who have lost the use of their legs can do any job they want to do.

☐ b. Debbie Graham would probably have died if she had been alone at the pool when she made her dive.

☐ c. When Debbie Graham first moved her hand, she cried because she was so sad.

2.

☐ a. If the Freehand System hadn't cost so much, it is likely that more people would have had it put in.

☐ b. Nichole is counting on being on a swim team soon.

☐ c. Debbie's, Todd's, and Nichole's brains didn't work the right way.

Score 4 points for each correct answer.

_____ **Total Score:** Making Inferences

D | Using Words

Put an X in the box next to the definition below that is closest in meaning to the underlined word.

1. Because his legs are <u>paralyzed</u>, Anson will never walk again.

☐ a. very strong and long

☐ b. tired because of hard exercise

☐ c. not able to feel or move

2. When I am <u>unable</u> to remember someone's name, I give up and just say, "Hello, there!"

☐ a. not said

☐ b. not easy

☐ c. not able

3. A <u>baby-sitting</u> job is perfect for Rita because she loves playing with children.

☐ a. taking care of young animals at the zoo

☐ b. taking care of children

☐ c. making clothes for children

4. When the cars in line ahead of her moved, Mrs. Jackson drove <u>forward</u> a few feet and then stopped again.

☐ a. toward the front

☐ b. toward the back

☐ c. toward the beginning

5. I felt bad when I lost your jacket. Now that I know how much you liked it, I feel even <u>worse</u>.

☐ a. more bad

☐ b. better

☐ c. very good

6. Marisa is out of school and has a job, so she is <u>independent</u> of her mother and father.

☐ a. needing a lot of help

☐ b. not needing help

☐ c. not able to give help

Score 4 points for each correct answer.

_____ **Total Score:** Using Words

E | Author's Approach

Put an X in the box next to the correct answer.

1. The main purpose of the first paragraph is to

☐ a. make people more careful when they swim.

☐ b. tell how the Freehand System works.

☐ c. tell how Debbie Graham became paralyzed.

2. What is the author's purpose in writing this article?

☐ a. to get the reader to see how helpful science can be

☐ b. to tell the reader how hard it is to pick up a glass without using your hands

☐ c. to explain how the body works to make our hands move

3. From the statements below, choose the one that you believe the author would agree with.

☐ a. Debbie, Todd, and Nichole were lucky to get the Freehand System put in them.

☐ b. The Freehand System is not worth much because it hurts too much to have it put in.

☐ c. Scientists could find better things to do than to find ways to help paralyzed people.

Score 4 points for each correct answer.

_____ **Total Score:** Author's Approach

F | Summarizing and Paraphrasing

Put an X in the box next to the correct answer.

1. Which summary says all the important things about the article?

☐ a. The Freehand System lets messages get from the brain to the hands. It helps people like Debbie Graham, Todd Anderson, and Nichole Good who can not move their hands. The system costs too much to make now.

☐ b. Debbie Graham, Todd Anderson, and Nichole Good can now pick up a glass. They had all been paralyzed. Debbie was hurt in a dive. Todd had a truck crash. And Nichole was in a car that hit a tree.

☐ c. People who get the Freehand System put in take a long time to heal. Debbie Graham spent three weeks in bed and two months getting stronger before she moved her hand.

2. Which sentence means the same thing as the following sentence? "But messages from their brains could no longer get to these hands."

☐ a. But messages from their hands were stopped before they got to their brains.

☐ b. But their brains didn't have messages for their hands.

☐ c. But their brains couldn't get messages to their hands anymore.

Score 4 points for each correct answer.

_____ **Total Score:** Summarizing and Paraphrasing

G | Critical Thinking

Put an X in the box next to the correct answer.

1. Choose the statement below that states a fact.

☐ a. Putting the Freehand System in took too long.

☐ b. Putting the Freehand System box in place took eight hours.

☐ c. Scientists should find a way to cut the cost of the Freehand System.

2. From information in the article, you can predict that

☐ a. doctors will start putting Freehand Systems into whoever wants them for free.

☐ b. scientists will keep working to find a way to help people who are paralyzed.

☐ c. no one else will need something like a Freehand System ever again.

3. Debbie, Todd, and Nichole are alike because

☐ a. they all wanted to be on swim teams.

☐ b. they could all move their shoulders.

☐ c. they were all 23 years old when they lost the use of their arms and legs.

4. What was the effect of the high cost of the Freehand System?

☐ a. No one wanted the system put in them.

☐ b. The system stopped working right.

☐ c. The system stopped being made or sold.

5. Which lesson about life does this story teach?

☐ a. You don't know how important some things are until they are taken away from you.

☐ b. You can always turn to your family for help when you are in trouble.

☐ c. If you wait long enough, your problems will go away by themselves.

Score 4 points for each correct answer.

_____ **Total Score:** Critical Thinking

Enter your score for each activity. Add the scores together. Record your total score on the graph on page 115.

_____ Finding the Main Idea

_____ Recalling Facts

_____ Making Inferences

_____ Using Words

_____ Author's Approach

_____ Summarizing and Paraphrasing

_____ Critical Thinking

_____ **Total Score**

Personal Response

What new question do you have about this topic?

_____

_____

Self-Assessment

From reading this article, I have learned _____

_____

Compare and Contrast

Pick two stories in Unit One that tell about something that people have made using science.
Use information from the stories to fill in this chart.

Title	What thing has been made?	What does the thing do?	Why do people like this thing?

Imagine that you were trying to sell one of these things. What would you say to make someone want to buy it? _____

_____

_____

UNIT TWO

How Fast Is Too Fast?

The signs are there. In big bright letters they warn everyone. "Do not ride if you have a weak heart. Do not ride if you have a bad neck. Do not ride if you have back problems." The list goes on and on. Still, people line up to get on these roller coaster rides. They can't wait to be scared half to death.

2 Every year roller coasters seem to get higher and go faster. Some are now over 200 feet high. They can go from zero to 80 miles an hour in less than three seconds. And they have all kinds of twists and turns. That's just what most people want. After riding one of these coasters, a girl shouted, "That was cool!" and a boy said, "It was amazing."

3 But some people are not so sure the new coasters are just "cool" and "amazing." They think they are a real danger to riders' health. In 2000 a young woman in Japan rode some of the fastest rides. One was a super-fast roller coaster. Later that day, her head began to hurt. Doctors found blood clots in her brain. This

Riders enjoy a topsy-turvy spin on the X-Flight roller coaster at an amusement park in Ohio.

woman was lucky. It took eight weeks, but her doctors fixed the problem.

4 What caused the blood clots? Dr. Toshio Fukutake said it might have been the roller coaster. He said it was rare for someone to get clots after riding a roller coaster. But "it can happen." The doctor said the roller coasters that are bigger and faster "may be more dangerous."

5 A second woman was not so lucky. In 2001 she rode a super-fast roller coaster in California. The ride lasted three minutes. Just after that, the 28-year-old-woman passed out. She was rushed to the hospital. It was too late. She died. It turned out that she, too, had blood clots. Did the ride cause the clots?

6 Edward Markey thinks it did. Markey is in the U.S. Congress. "This is a rapidly growing problem," he says. Markey wants laws to control how high and how fast the new rides can be.

7 What does a roller coaster ride do to the body? One way to answer that question is to look at the g-force. That shows how much force a person feels as he or she changes speed or direction. Changing speed raises the g-force. So does changing direction. That's because everything in the body gets pushed forward, backward, or to the side. This includes the blood. As the g-force goes up, so does the danger. Markey wants to limit how much g-force a ride can have.

8   In 2002 experts studied roller coasters and their g-forces. They found it "unlikely" that the rides hurt the brain. These same experts pointed out that the old roller coasters went slower, but they had tight turns. The new roller coasters are faster. But they have much wider turns. So there is little difference in the g-force of the old and new coasters.

9   What are g-forces like in everyday life? Most of the time, people stay at a g-force of one. A cough can put you at a g-force of three. But that only lasts a split second. The same is true if you jump down off a high step. You might feel a g-force of eight. But it's gone in the blink of an eye. Pilots in F-16 fighter jets, on the other hand, may face a g-force of nine. And it may last 10 or 20 seconds.

10   Dr. Douglas Smith is an expert in the field. He says pillow fights put more force on the brain than roller coaster rides. Even the wildest ride does not have a g-force of more than five. Smith says that lots of people just have weak blood vessels in their brains. These could start to bleed at any time. It might happen while walking down the street. It might happen during sleep. It could happen on a roller coaster too. But Smith says that does not mean the ride itself is to blame.

11   Others aren't so sure. They think more studies should be done. Dr. Robert Braksiek says that roller coasters can hurt riders' brains. He adds, "Although rare, it does happen."

12   Even if roller coasters don't hurt the brain, they can still be dangerous. Other bad things can happen. Look at the Steel Dragon in Japan. In 2003 something went wrong with it. The coaster was going 30 miles an hour. Suddenly, one of its cars ran off the track. A young rider hurt her back. Meanwhile, several wheels broke loose from the roller coaster. One flew 100 feet through the air. It hit a man in a nearby swimming pool. He lived, but he was badly hurt.

13   Even a low and fairly slow ride like Disneyland's Big Thunder Mountain can be hazardous. In 2003, 22-year-old Marcelo Torres was on this ride. One of the cars came off the track and hit the car he was in. Torres was killed. Ten others were hurt.

14   So again, read the warning signs. You ride at your own risk. The new coasters are built to be safe. But even with the safest roller coaster, there is always risk. As one expert said, "Moving human bodies rapidly through space is not risk-free."

A | Finding the Main Idea

One statement below tells the main idea of the article. One statement is too general, or too broad. The other statement explains only part of the article; it is too narrow. Label the statements using the following key:

M—Main Idea   **B—Too Broad**   **N—Too Narrow**

_____ 1. Though roller coasters are fun, they can also be dangerous because of their speed. Some people have died or gotten hurt by roller coasters.

_____ 2. Edward Markey, a member of the U.S. Congress, wants to limit how high and how fast a roller coaster can go. He says that high g-forces are too dangerous for riders.

_____ 3. Often, things that are fun also carry some danger. Even though people know that an action may hurt or even kill them, they sometimes choose to do it anyway.

Score 4 points for each correct answer.

_____ **Total Score:** Finding the Main Idea

B | Recalling Facts

How well do you remember the facts in the article? Put an X in the box next to the answer that correctly completes each statement.

1. After a young woman in Japan rode a super-fast roller coaster, doctors found
   ☐ a. problems with her heart.
   ☐ b. blood clots in her brain.
   ☐ c. that her muscles had become weak.

2. The author says that g-force is
   ☐ a. the force a person feels when changing speed or direction.
   ☐ b. the force of something hitting a person at great speed.
   ☐ c. the force that takes a roller coaster up a hill.

3. In 2003 a wheel flew off the Steel Dragon roller coaster. It
   ☐ a. hit a young rider in the back and hurt her badly.
   ☐ b. gave a young woman a blood clot.
   ☐ c. hit a man in a nearby swimming pool.

4. Marcelo Torres was killed when
   ☐ a. he got a blood clot after riding roller coaster.
   ☐ b. another roller coaster car hit the car he was riding in.
   ☐ c. his roller coaster car jumped off its track and fell.

Score 4 points for each correct answer.

_____ **Total Score:** Recalling Facts

C | Making Inferences

When you draw a conclusion that is not directly stated in the text, you are making an inference. Put an X in the box next to the statement that is a correct inference.

1.

☐ a. If people really believed that roller coasters could be dangerous, no one would ride them.

☐ b. People who run roller coasters believe that roller coasters are safe for all but a few people.

☐ c. Riding a roller coaster is perfectly safe for people who are feeling well.

2.

☐ a. Any ride that jerks riders around fast and hard probably has a high g-force.

☐ b. People with weak hearts or back problems cannot get on roller coasters.

☐ c. If there were even a small chance the roller coasters were dangerous, companies would stop making them.

Score 4 points for each correct answer.

_____ **Total Score:** Making Inferences

D | Using Words

Put an X in the box next to the definition below that is closest in meaning to the underlined word or phrase.

1. Riders on a <u>roller coaster</u> can be lifted off their seats for a moment when the car goes down a hill fast.

☐ a. a ride in which cars on tracks go up and down suddenly

☐ b. a ride in which cars go around on a giant wheel

☐ c. a ride in which wooden horses go around and around

2. To keep our <u>health</u>, we should eat right and exercise often.

☐ a. the state of feeling sick

☐ b. the state of feeling well

☐ c. the state of feeling scared

3. The old milk had formed so many <u>clots</u> that it poured out of the bottle in chunks.

☐ a. holes in a tube, bottle, or box

☐ b. groups of water drops floating in the sky

☐ c. lumps in a liquid

4. It is important that our <u>blood vessels</u> stay clear so our blood can flow freely.

☐ a. jars of blood given to people who are hurt and bleeding

☐ b. tubes that carry blood through the body

☐ c. people who put blood in the body of a person who has lost too much blood

5. Police say that the roads are icy and <u>hazardous</u>. So to stay safe, we won't drive anywhere.

☐ a. natural
☐ b. beautiful
☐ c. dangerous

6. A dangerous sport such as mountain climbing carries some <u>risk</u>. If you climb, you should be ready for trouble.

☐ a. time for fun and friends
☐ b. sure feeling of safety
☐ c. chance of failing or getting hurt

> Score 4 points for each correct answer.
>
> _____ **Total Score:** Using Words

E | Author's Approach

Put an X in the box next to the correct answer.

1. What is the author's purpose in writing this article?

☐ a. to get readers to stop riding roller coasters
☐ b. to tell readers that roller coasters might be dangerous
☐ c. to show that roller coasters in Japan are more dangerous than the ones in the United States

2. Choose the statement below that best describes the author's opinion in paragraph 1.

☐ a. Many people like to do risky things.
☐ b. People who run roller coasters don't care about keeping riders safe.
☐ c. People who run roller coasters don't do enough to let riders know the ride may be dangerous.

3. The author says that Dr. Douglas Smith is not sure that roller coasters are to blame when blood vessels in a brain bleed after a ride. Choose the statement below that best explains how the author deals with the opposite point of view.

☐ a. The author says that Edward Markey wants to limit the g-force that roller coasters can have.
☐ b. The author points out that some people have been hurt when roller coasters go off their tracks.
☐ c. The author points out that Dr. Robert Braksiek has said that roller coasters can and do hurt riders' brains.

> Score 4 points for each correct answer.
>
> _____ **Total Score:** Author's Approach

F Summarizing and Paraphrasing

Put an X in the box next to the correct answer.

1. Which summary says all the important things about the article?

☐ a. In 2003, a roller coaster car ran off its track in Japan. At least two people were hurt. In the same year, a roller coaster car ran off the track at Disneyland. A young man lost his life in this accident.

☐ b. Most of the time, people feel a g-force of one. Even a simple action such as a cough raises the g-force to three. Experts say that the g-force of a wild roller coaster is about five.

☐ c. People might have gotten deadly blood clots from riding on roller coasters. Not all experts agree that is true. But it is true that people have been hurt by these rides in other ways.

2. Which sentence means the same thing as the following sentence? "But it's gone in the blink of an eye."

☐ a. But it leaves very quickly.
☐ b. But it takes a long time to leave.
☐ c. But you can hardly tell that it's gone.

Score 4 points for each correct answer.

_____ **Total Score:** Summarizing and Paraphrasing

G Critical Thinking

Put an X in the box next to the correct answer.

1. Choose the statement below that states an opinion.

☐ a. Some roller coasters are 200 feet high.
☐ b. Roller coasters are the most dangerous rides you can go on.
☐ c. In 2001 a young woman who had just ridden a roller coaster passed out and soon died.

2. From information in the article, you can predict that

☐ a. people who run roller coasters will keep warning riders about possible dangers.
☐ b. very soon, no one will want to ride any roller coaster.
☐ c. soon, experts will agree that roller coasters are perfectly safe for everyone.

3. Old roller coasters and newer roller coasters are different because

☐ a. the newer roller coasters have much higher g-forces than the older ones.
☐ b. newer roller coasters cost less to build than the older ones.
☐ c. the older roller coasters went slower and had tighter turns than the newer ones.

4. In which paragraph did you find the information or details to answer question 3?

☐ a. paragraph 7
☐ b. paragraph 8
☐ c. paragraph 9

5. Which lesson about life does this story teach?

☐ a. Everything that is fun is also dangerous.

☐ b. Nothing that is dangerous can ever be fun.

☐ c. Some things that are fun can be dangerous.

Score 4 points for each correct answer.

_____ **Total Score:** Critical Thinking

Enter your score for each activity. Add the scores together. Record your total score on the graph on page 115.

_____ Finding the Main Idea

_____ Recalling Facts

_____ Making Inferences

_____ Using Words

_____ Author's Approach

_____ Summarizing and Paraphrasing

_____ Critical Thinking

_____ **Total Score**

Personal Response

What was most surprising or interesting to you about this article? _____

_____

Self-Assessment

One good question about this article that was not asked would be " _____

_____ ?"

A Police Officer's Best Friend

It's not very tall—less than four feet high. It's not very wide—only about a foot and a half. And it's not very fast. Its top speed is less than four miles an hour. Still, it is the new best friend of many police officers. Its name is Andros F6A, and it is a new robot used by police across the country.

2   Andros can do all sorts of cool things. It can roll across grass or soft sand. It can cross a muddy field dotted with deep holes. It can climb stairs. It can walk down the aisle in an airplane. It can move tables and chairs. It can even open a door and knock out windows.

3   But that's not all. Andros has its own eyes and ears. The robot has four cameras mounted on it. These let police see whatever the robot sees. One camera is a special night camera. So Andros—and the police who are watching—can see in the dark. Andros has a microphone to capture sound. This microphone is very strong. It can even hear a pin drop.

4   If there's trouble, Andros can handle it. The robot can check people's bags for guns or knives. It can test

Pictured here is Andros F6A, a new robot that police are using. The robot can help them do all sorts of jobs.

the air to see whether there is any poison in it. Andros's long arm can knock a gun out of a person's hand. It can use its arm to drag a person away from danger. Andros can shoot pepper spray. It can send out a net to capture someone. It can blast someone with a powerful jet stream of water. The robot can even shoot rubber bullets. And Andros is armed with real guns in case a person puts up a hard fight.

5   With all these tricks up its sleeve, Andros is not cheap. One of these robots costs well over $100,000. But that seems like a small price to pay for someone's life. And Andros does save lives. The police can send Andros to do all sorts of dangerous jobs. Suppose the police think a box has a bomb in it. They could send a human to find out. But what if the box blows up? The blast might kill a human. With Andros, an officer can stand 500 feet away. From that safe distance, he or she can control every move the robot makes. Of course, a big blast might hurt the robot. But that's okay. As Officer Bob Lewis says, "It's easier to replace a robot arm than a person."

6   In March 2002, police in Dundalk, Maryland, found another use for Andros. A man named Joseph Palczynski was on the loose. Police suspected him of killing four people. Now he was holding three other people inside a house. Police told Palczynski to give himself up. He refused.

7　　As the hours passed, Palczynski got more and more upset. He got tired and hungry too. He said he would kill the people in the house. Police knew they had to calm him down. They wanted to send in food. But he was so angry that he might have killed anyone who came to the house. So the police called on Andros. The robot came and delivered a pizza to Palczynski. Without risking any officer's life, Andros got the job done. And in the end, all three people being held got out safely.

8　　It's no wonder police love their robots. Some even give them names. Police in Springfield, Oregon, call their robot Big Jim. About 60 times a year, Big Jim is used to check out possible bombs. In February 2004, it was called to help handle a man with a gun. The man was holed up inside a building. He had just shot a woman. When the police came, he began to shoot at them, too. One officer was hit. There was no way to know what the man might do next. The police knew they had to get into the building and get the gun away from him. But they didn't know what the inside of the building looked like. Where were the doorways? Where was the man himself? Had he set any traps for them? If the police burst in, he could kill them before they had a chance.

9　　Clearly, this was a case for Big Jim Andros. The police did not report exactly what Andros did. But the robot did get in the building. And 10 minutes later, police entered and captured the man.

10　　Andros can't solve every problem, of course. Humans are still needed. In fact, it takes skilled humans to run Andros in the first place. There are buttons to push and controls to turn. There are cameras to watch. If police aren't careful, the 350-pound robot could topple over. Then it would be worthless. So Andros is only as good as the person running it. Officers spend five weeks training before they can use Andros. And as Officer Ralph Burks says, "It's a skill that you can lose. We do training throughout the year. We all take turns working the robot."

11　　The officers don't mind the extra training. They know how important Andros is to them. As Officer Marc Smith put it, "This is one of the greatest tools we've got." ✎

A | Finding the Main Idea

One statement below tells the main idea of the article. One statement is too general, or too broad. The other statement explains only part of the article; it is too narrow. Label the statements using the following key:

M—Main Idea   B—Too Broad   N—Too Narrow

_____ 1. Police have a difficult job to do. Anything that can help them do their job better and more safely is welcome.

_____ 2. When police have a dangerous job to do, many now use a robot named Andros F6A. This robot can get the job done without risking any officer's life.

_____ 3. Andros can do many dangerous jobs. It can look for guns, and it can knock a gun out of someone's hand. It can check the air for poison. It can shoot out a powerful stream of water.

Score 4 points for each correct answer.

_____ **Total Score:** Finding the Main Idea

B | Recalling Facts

How well do you remember the facts in the article? Put an X in the box next to the answer that correctly completes each statement.

1. Andros F6A costs about
   - ☐ a. $1,000.
   - ☐ b. $100,000.
   - ☐ c. $1,000,000.

2. When Joseph Palczynski was holding three people inside a house in Dundalk, Maryland, Andros helped the police by
   - ☐ a. knocking the gun from his hand.
   - ☐ b. delivering pizza to him.
   - ☐ c. shooting a rubber bullet at Palczynski.

3. Police in Springfield, Oregon, call their robot
   - ☐ a. Big Jim.
   - ☐ b. Rover.
   - ☐ c. Big Gene.

4. Before an officer can run Andros, he or she must train for
   - ☐ a. one full year.
   - ☐ b. six months.
   - ☐ c. five weeks.

Score 4 points for each correct answer.

_____ **Total Score:** Recalling Facts

59

C Making Inferences

When you draw a conclusion that is not directly stated in the text, you are making an inference. Put an X in the box next to the statement that is a correct inference.

1.

☐ a. If Andros hadn't helped the police in Dundalk, Palczynski might have killed the three people he held in a house.

☐ b. If Palczynski had stolen Andros, he could quickly have figured out how to use the robot against the police.

☐ c. When someone is upset, he or she is never interested in eating any food.

2.

☐ a. The best police force would be made up of lots of Andros robots and just one person.

☐ b. It would be easy for Andros to catch up with someone who was driving away from it.

☐ c. Police in Springfield, Oregon, deal with more than 50 possible bombs each year.

Score 4 points for each correct answer.

_____ **Total Score:** Making Inferences

D Using Words

Put an X in the box next to the definition below that is closest in meaning to the underlined word.

1. We walked down the center <u>aisle</u> at the theater and looked for four seats together.

☐ a. the middle part of a street or road
☐ b. a rocky path used for hiking through a forest
☐ c. an open way to walk between groups of seats

2. Speak into the <u>microphone</u> so everyone can hear you.

☐ a. a tool for picking up small sounds and making them louder
☐ b. a tool that people use to see tiny things and make them seem bigger
☐ c. a tool that allows people to send messages using a code of electric signals

3. The notebooks at that store were <u>cheap</u>, so I bought enough to last the rest of the year.

☐ a. not costing much
☐ b. costing too much
☐ c. not the right size

4. Mr. Wright is looking for a <u>skilled</u> carpenter to build a deck on his house.

☐ a. not interested in doing anything
☐ b. not able to do anything well
☐ c. able to do something well

5. If you push it, the tower of blocks will <u>topple</u>.

☐ a. stand straighter
☐ b. fall over
☐ c. grow taller

6. Wet matches are <u>worthless</u> for lighting a fire.

☐ a. very useful
☐ b. of no use
☐ c. well known

Score 4 points for each correct answer.

_____ **Total Score:** Using Words

E Author's Approach

Put an X in the box next to the correct answer.

1. The main purpose of the first paragraph is to

☐ a. prove that the Andros F6A costs too much.
☐ b. show how the Andros F6A can help police.
☐ c. describe the Andros F6A.

2. Choose the statement below that best describes the author's opinion in paragraph 2.

☐ a. Andros can't do much that is worth doing.
☐ b. Andros does some wonderful things.
☐ c. Andros does what people do, only not as well.

3. The author probably wrote this article in order to

☐ a. tell how the Andros F6A can be used.
☐ b. get police to buy Andros F6A robots.
☐ c. show how brave police officers are.

Score 4 points for each correct answer.

_____ **Total Score:** Author's Approach

F | Summarizing and Paraphrasing

Put an X in the box next to the correct answer.

1. Which summary says all the important things about the article?

☐ a. The Andros robot has a microphone. The microphone helps people working the robot hear what is happening around it. People running Andros can also see what the robot sees by looking at pictures taken by its four cameras.

☐ b. Police in Springfield, Oregon, used the Andros robot one time to capture a man with a gun. Andros was able to get into the building where the man was holed up. A few minutes later, police officers were able to take the man safely.

☐ c. Police officers like using a robot called Andros F6A. It can do things they cannot do. It can be sent into places where police officers could be killed. To use Andros well, police must be trained in how to control it.

2. Which sentence means the same thing as the following sentence? "It's no wonder police love their robots."

☐ a. No one knows why police love their robots.
☐ b. It's easy to understand why police love their robots.
☐ c. The way the police love their robots is wonderful.

Score 4 points for each correct answer.

_____ **Total Score:** Summarizing and Paraphrasing

G | Critical Thinking

Put an X in the box next to the correct answer.

1. Choose the statement below that states a fact.

☐ a. Every police department should have at least two Andros robots.
☐ b. Andros is the best tool that the police have ever had.
☐ c. Andros has four cameras that let the police see what it sees.

2. From information in the article, you can predict that

☐ a. police will keep using Andros or robots that are like it for a long time.
☐ b. police will soon decide that Andros costs too much and will stop using it.
☐ c. soon, the only police officers will be robots like Andros.

3. Police officers and Andros are different because

☐ a. Andros can drag people away from danger.
☐ b. Andros's parts can be replaced if they are hurt.
☐ c. police officers can shoot rubber bullets.

4. Which paragraphs provide information that supports your answer to question 3?

☐ a. paragraphs 1 and 2
☐ b. paragraphs 4 and 5
☐ c. paragraphs 6 and 7

5. How is Andros an example of cool science?

☐ a. Police all over the country are starting to use Andros.

☐ b. Andros costs a lot, but it is worth the cost.

☐ c. Scientists made Andros, and it can do amazing things.

Score 4 points for each correct answer.

_____ **Total Score:** Critical Thinking

Enter your score for each activity. Add the scores together. Record your total score on the graph on page 115.

_____ Finding the Main Idea

_____ Recalling Facts

_____ Making Inferences

_____ Using Words

_____ Author's Approach

_____ Summarizing and Paraphrasing

_____ Critical Thinking

_____ **Total Score**

Personal Response

If you could ask the author of the article one question, what would it be? _____

_____

_____

Self-Assessment

When reading the article, I was having trouble with

_____

Journey to Saturn

After 15 years, it was finally ready to go. The spacecraft called *Cassini* was about to blast off from Florida. Scientists around the world held their breath. Would *Cassini* get off to a good start? Would its flight go smoothly? Would it stay on its course toward the distant planet Saturn?

2   Other spacecraft had gone near Saturn. But *Cassini* would do more. If all went well, it would go into orbit around the planet. Also, *Cassini* carried a special machine. It is called a "probe." This probe could pull away from the main spacecraft. It could then explore Titan, Saturn's largest moon.

3   Getting *Cassini* to Saturn was a mammoth job. The United States did not do it alone. Europe's space programs helped. So did people from 17 other countries. Parts came from all over the world. More than 8,000 scientists and workers pitched in. So when *Cassini* took off, the whole world really was watching.

Shown here is a drawing of the Cassini *spacecraft as it reached Saturn. The* Cassini *mission was a big success.*

4   The big event took place on October 15, 1997.

5   "It was a perfect launch," said one expert.

6   As *Cassini* sailed through space, people turned their eyes toward Saturn. It is one of the brightest things in the night sky. So humans have known about it for thousands of years. People were watching it long before they had telescopes. The ancient Romans saw it. In fact, they gave it its name. They called it "Saturn" after their god of farming.

7   Over the years, scientists have learned more and more about this mysterious planet. For one thing, they learned that it has many moons. They also learned that Saturn is very big. More than 750 Earths could fit inside it. On the other hand, Saturn is not as solid as Earth. Mostly it is made up of gases. It has no surface that someone could stand on. And it is so light that it would float in water.

8   Saturn is probably best known for its rings. These were first seen back in the 1650s. A Dutch scientist looked through his telescope and described Saturn as having a ring. His name was Christaan Huygens [HOY-ginz]. Soon after that, an Italian scientist saw that Saturn really had two main groups of rings. This scientist was Giovanni Cassini. Both of these men were honored in special ways in the mission to Saturn.

(A mission is a special job that people or things like spacecraft are sent to do.) The spacecraft was named *Cassini*. And the probe was named *Huygens*.

9   It took *Cassini* almost seven years to reach Saturn. At last, on June 30, 2004, the spacecraft arrived at its destination. It passed through the rings of Saturn. And it began to orbit the planet.

10   Back on Earth, scientists cheered. They had done it! They had gotten the spacecraft to Saturn! *Cassini* would spend the next four years orbiting the planet. In that time, people would get a good close look at Saturn. *Cassini* has lots of cameras. Some are very strong. One can see a small coin from two miles away. *Cassini* will take 300,000 pictures. And right from the start, the pictures were astounding.

11   "I've been working on this mission for 14 years," said Dr. Carolyn Porco. "And I shouldn't be surprised." Still, Porco said she found the pictures "shocking." She could not believe how clear and beautiful they were.

12   As scientists had hoped, the pictures showed things never seen before. People had thought Saturn had 31 moons. *Cassini* quickly found two more. And that was just the beginning. *Cassini* checked out Saturn's rings. Scientists knew the rings were cold. Everything in them was frozen. But what exactly were they made of?

Experts expected *Cassini* to find dirt and ice in the rings. It did. But it found that the chunks of ice at the outer edge of the rings were clean. The ones closer to the planet were filled with dirt. It also found rocks in the space between the rings. Scientists would spend years figuring out what all this meant. Did the rocks come from moons that had broken apart? If not, where did the rocks come from? And why was the ice cleaner at the far edge of the rings?

13   And then there is *Huygens*. This probe has its own special part to play. On Christmas Eve, 2004, it would leave *Cassini*. Twenty-two days later, it would land on the moon Titan. Scientists feel this could be one of the best parts of the whole mission. Titan is about the size of Earth. It is probably too cold to have life. But in other ways, it may be a lot like Earth. It might help us understand what Earth was like before life began here. Does it rain on Titan? Are there lakes or rivers? How strong is the wind? These are among the questions scientists hope *Hugyens* would answer.

14   By the fall of 2004, the *Cassini* mission was clearly a success. Many mysteries remain about Saturn. But we now know more than ever before about this "Jewel of the Solar System." 🎗

A | Finding the Main Idea

One statement below tells the main idea of the article. One statement is too general, or too broad. The other statement explains only part of the article; it is too narrow. Label the statements using the following key:

M—Main Idea   **B—Too Broad**   **N—Too Narrow**

_____ 1. *Cassini* told scientists that Saturn has 33 moons. *Cassini* also told scientists that the ice in the rings closest to Saturn are dirtier than the ice in the rings farthest away from it.

_____ 2. For many years, humans have been curious about the planet called Saturn. They had to study it from far away. Now they are learning more than they have even known.

_____ 3. In 1997 a spacecraft called *Cassini* was sent to Saturn. It arrived there in 2004. Its job is to learn more about Saturn and its rings. Another job is to send a probe to look at Titan, a moon of Saturn.

Score 4 points for each correct answer.

_____ **Total Score:** Finding the Main Idea

B | Recalling Facts

How well do you remember the facts in the article? Put an X in the box next to the answer that correctly completes each statement.

1. Saturn was named after the

☐ a. Roman god of farming.
☐ b. scientist who first saw the planet.
☐ c. Greek god of war.

2. Saturn's rings were first seen in the

☐ a. 1400s.
☐ b. 1650s.
☐ c. 1900s.

3. The probe *Huygens* was named after

☐ a. the scientist who first saw Saturn.
☐ b. the scientist who planned the spacecraft's mission.
☐ c. the scientist who first saw Saturn's rings.

4. On June 30, 2004, the *Cassini*

☐ a. landed on planet Saturn.
☐ b. landed on the moon Titan.
☐ c. went into orbit around Saturn.

Score 4 points for each correct answer.

_____ **Total Score:** Recalling Facts

C | Making Inferences

When you draw a conclusion that is not directly stated in the text, you are making an inference. Put an X in the box next to the statement that is a correct inference.

1.

☐ a. Scientists are the only people curious about Saturn, its rings, and its moons.

☐ b. Saturn is very far from Earth.

☐ c. Humans could easily build cities on Saturn.

2.

☐ a. It would be possible to walk on the rings of Saturn.

☐ b. Only missions that a single country works on can be successes.

☐ c. Before 1650, most telescopes were not strong enough to see Saturn clearly.

Score 4 points for each correct answer.

_____ **Total Score:** Making Inferences

D | Using Words

Put an X in the box next to the definition below that is closest in meaning to the underlined word.

1. After flying at top speed for seven years, the <u>spacecraft</u> reached Saturn.

☐ a. a ship that flies through space

☐ b. a suit that people wear in space

☐ c. a person who explores space

2. The spaceship's <u>orbit</u> was hundreds of miles above the planet.

☐ a. the rocket that takes a ship into space

☐ b. the person who controls a spaceship

☐ c. the path a spaceship flies on around a planet

3. No one could move the <u>mammoth</u> rock that had fallen from the mountain top.

☐ a. tiny

☐ b. huge

☐ c. secret

4. Many people watched the TV to see the <u>launch</u> of the rocket into space.

☐ a. a type of metal used in rockets

☐ b. the time of day just before night

☐ c. the act of sending off

5. When the plane reached its <u>destination</u>, all the passengers got off.

☐ a. the place someone or something is leaving
☐ b. the place someone or something is going toward
☐ c. a place that is hard to find

6. It is <u>astounding</u> that you would spend so much money on something that is worth so little.

☐ a. very surprising
☐ b. natural
☐ c. lucky

Score 4 points for each correct answer.

_____ **Total Score:** Using Words

E | Author's Approach

Put an X in the box next to the correct answer.

1. What is the author's purpose in writing this article?

☐ a. to tell about a mission to study Saturn and Titan
☐ b. to tell why people should explore Saturn
☐ c. to make readers afraid of what might happen to *Cassini*

2. From the statements below, choose the one that you believe the author would agree with.

☐ a. *Cassini* and *Huygens* should have been sent to Saturn many years ago.
☐ b. It will be interesting to see what *Cassini* and *Huygens* tell us about Saturn and Titan.
☐ c. It would be enough just to study Saturn's rings; studying Titan doesn't need to be done too.

3. Choose the statement below that best describes the author's opinion in paragraph 7.

☐ a. We know almost nothing about Saturn.
☐ b. Saturn is a better planet than Earth.
☐ c. Saturn is very different from Earth.

Score 4 points for each correct answer.

_____ **Total Score:** Author's Approach

F | Summarizing and Paraphrasing

Put an X in the box next to the correct answer.

1. Which summary says all the important things about the article?

☐ a. The *Cassini* spacecraft, launched in 1997 and reaching Saturn in 2004, is teaching us much about Saturn. *Cassini* is sending back clear pictures of the planet. It is also sending information about Saturn's rings. The probe *Huygens*'s job is to study Saturn's moon Titan.

☐ b. Scientists and workers from 18 nations worked on the *Cassini* mission. The U.S. space program and Europe's space programs worked together. About 8,000 people from all over the world helped, too.

☐ c. It took seven years for the spacecraft *Cassini* to reach Saturn. Although other spacecraft had gone near Saturn before, this was the first one to orbit it. The *Cassini* was named for a scientist of long ago.

2. Which sentence means the same thing as the following sentence? "Scientists around the world held their breath."

☐ a. Scientists all over the world stopped talking.

☐ b. Scientists from every country were not pleased by what was about to happen.

☐ c. All over the world, scientists waited to see what would happen.

Score 4 points for each correct answer.

_____ **Total Score:** Summarizing and Paraphrasing

G | Critical Thinking

Put an X in the box next to the correct answer.

1. Choose the statement below that states an opinion.

☐ a. More than 750 Earths could fit inside Saturn.

☐ b. More than 8,000 people helped to get *Cassini* to Saturn.

☐ c. Getting the *Cassini* to Saturn was worth all the time and money spent.

2. From information in the article, one can predict that

☐ a. nothing much will be learned from this mission.

☐ b. scientists around the world will share what they learn from this mission.

☐ c. one day we will find out that humans lived on Saturn.

3. Earth and Saturn are different because

☐ a. Earth has more moons than Saturn has.

☐ b. Earth is much bigger than Saturn.

☐ c. only Saturn is made up mostly of gases.

4. In which paragraph did you find the information or details to answer question 3?

☐ a. paragraph 6

☐ b. paragraph 7

☐ c. paragraph 8

5. How is the *Cassini* mission related to cool science?

☐ a. Without science, we wouldn't have this great way to learn more about the world we live in.

☐ b. Because of science, the planet Saturn has interesting rings.

☐ c. There is much that we don't know about the planet Saturn.

Score 4 points for each correct answer.

_____ **Total Score:** Critical Thinking

Enter your score for each activity. Add the scores together. Record your total score on the graph on page 115.

_____ Finding the Main Idea

_____ Recalling Facts

_____ Making Inferences

_____ Using Words

_____ Author's Approach

_____ Summarizing and Paraphrasing

_____ Critical Thinking

_____ **Total Score**

Personal Response

What new question do you have about this topic?

_____

_____

Self-Assessment

Before reading this article, I already knew _____

_____

Lost and Found

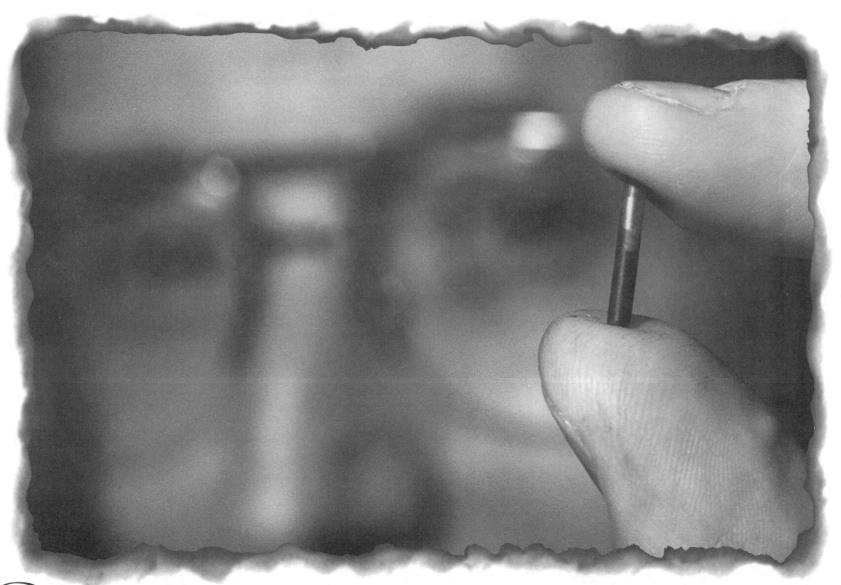

Bambi Lesne thought it sounded like a great plan. "That way," she said to herself, "if anything happens, I can get her back."

2   Bambi was thinking about her new puppy, a tiny Pomeranian. Most people put collars on their dogs. These have tags that give the owner's address. But Bambi knew that collars can get lost. She had something else in mind. It is called a microchip. This tiny computer chip can be put under the skin at the base of a dog's neck. Each chip has a code number. The code tells who the dog's owner is.

3   It was 1989 when Bambi got the microchip for her puppy. She had it put in at the Humane Society of Bay County in Florida. Then Bambi settled in to life with her new pet. She loved her little Pooh Bear. So did Bambi's daughter Codi. Pooh Bear was so small she could fit into a small beach bag. Codi took Pooh Bear all around town in the bag. She even taught the dog to jump into the bag without help.

Shown here is a microchip that is put under a pet's skin. The microchip has a code number that tells who owns the dog.

4   Bambi said Pooh Bear "was the best dog I ever had." She added, "She never barked. She never was a bad dog." For seven years, Pooh Bear lived happily with the Lesne family. "She went everywhere with us. She was like one of my children," said Bambi.

5   Then, in 1996, Pooh Bear disappeared. Was she stolen? Did she just wander off? Bambi didn't know. But she was miserable. She cried whenever she thought of Pooh Bear. She put lost dog notices in newspapers. She called all the dog shelters near her home. For three years she searched. Finally she gave up hope of ever seeing Pooh Bear again.

6   Three more years passed. Then, on July 5, 2002, something astonishing happened. A woman named Peggy spotted a dog in Cincinnati, Ohio. It was running through the streets. The dog was in pretty sad shape. Its fur was dirty, and its teeth were bad. Peggy took the dog home and gave it a bath. Then she took it to an animal doctor. Dr. Cheryl Devine checked to see whether the dog had a microchip. It did. The doctor then traced the number back to the Humane Society of Bay County. The records were clear. The dog was Pooh Bear!

7   A woman from the Society called Bambi. "You're not going to believe this," she said. "You remember that little black dog you had? She was running the streets of Cincinnati!"

8 Bambi was stunned. It had been six years since Pooh Bear had vanished. Was it really possible that she had been found after all this time? And Cincinnati was 600 miles away. How in the world had Pooh Bear ended up there? Bambi wanted to make sure this was her dog. She called Peggy and asked a key question. "Does the dog's tiny nose turn up just a little bit?"

9 The answer, of course, was yes. Pooh Bear was now 13 years old. She had some gray hairs and a scar on her head. But thanks to the microchip, there was no doubt about it. This was Pooh Bear.

10 Peggy offered to fly the dog down to Florida and give her to Bambi in person. It's no wonder that Bambi calls Peggy "the greatest woman in the world." Within a couple of days, Pooh Bear was back in Bambi's arms. It was like old times again. One of the first things Pooh Bear did was to jump into Codi's beach bag.

11 Dr. Devine was very happy with the way the microchip system had worked. She said it was "exciting." "You always hope they'll have a chip. But you never expect them to have one."

12 There's a reason why Devine doesn't expect pets to have the microchips. The United States may lead the world in using many new things. But that's not true when it comes to microchips for pets. The chips first went on sale in the late 1980s. But 15 years later, less than 4 percent of America's dogs and cats had them.

13 Some owners just don't know about the chip. Others think it costs too much. That is not true. In fact, it costs less than $60 to have a microchip put in a pet. That's about what people pay for a good collar and tag.

14 Some people think that it will hurt their pet to have the chip put in. It won't. The animal feels only a tiny pinch. Bonnie McErlane had chips put into her two dogs. "Nobody cried; nobody got upset," she said. Then she added jokingly, "Not even me."

15 In other countries, the chip is more widely used. In Australia all dogs must have a microchip. It's the law. In France and England, no dog can be brought into the country without one. There is no law about microchips in the United States. But Bambi Lesne knows that without a chip, her little Pooh Bear would have been lost to her forever.

A | Finding the Main Idea

One statement below tells the main idea of the article. One statement is too general, or too broad. The other statement explains only part of the article; it is too narrow. Label the statements using the following key:

M—Main Idea   B—Too Broad   N—Too Narrow

_____ 1. Bambi Lesne got a little dog that she named Pooh Bear. At the Humane Society of Bay County in Florida, she had a microchip with a code put into her dog.

_____ 2. People were able to find the owner of a lost dog named Pooh Bear because of a microchip put into it. Although these microchips are often used in other countries, pets in the United States hardly ever get them.

_____ 3. People love their pets. When a pet goes missing, the pet owner is usually upset. A good way to match up lost pets and their owners has been found.

Score 4 points for each correct answer.

_____ **Total Score:** Finding the Main Idea

B | Recalling Facts

How well do you remember the facts in the article? Put an X in the box next to the answer that correctly completes each statement.

1. After Pooh Bear disappeared, Bambi Lesne
   - ☐ a. looked for the dog for three years.
   - ☐ b. forgot about the dog right away and got a new one.
   - ☐ c. drove to Cincinnati to look for it.

2. Pooh Bear was found in Cincinnati
   - ☐ a. three years after she disappeared.
   - ☐ b. six years after she disappeared.
   - ☐ c. ten years after she disappeared.

3. The person who found the microchip in Pooh Bear was
   - ☐ a. the woman who found Pooh Bear on the street.
   - ☐ b. a worker at the Humane Society.
   - ☐ c. an animal doctor.

4. Without a microchip, a dog may not be brought into
   - ☐ a. Mexico and Russia.
   - ☐ b. France and England.
   - ☐ c. Canada and the United States.

Score 4 points for each correct answer.

_____ **Total Score:** Recalling Facts

C | Making Inferences

When you draw a conclusion that is not directly stated in the text, you are making an inference. Put an X in the box next to the statement that is a correct inference.

1.

☐ a. After years of looking for Pooh Bear, Bambi probably didn't care if she saw the dog ever again.

☐ b. Bambi Lesne would probably tell other pet owners to get microchips put into their pets.

☐ c. Dogs can't remember people for more than a few days.

2.

☐ a. If pet owners knew more about microchips, more of them would get the microchips put into their pets.

☐ b. People who don't get microchips put into their pets don't really care about their pets' safety.

☐ c. Putting a microchip into a pet is the only way to get the pet back if it runs away.

Score 4 points for each correct answer.

_____ **Total Score:** Making Inferences

D | Using Words

Put an X in the box next to the definition below that is closest in meaning to the underlined word.

1. The company has made a new <u>microchip</u> that will help computers work faster.

☐ a. a little snack food, such as a potato chip

☐ b. a small but important part of a computer

☐ c. a very small animal

2. That such a little dog could travel hundreds of miles on its own is <u>astonishing</u>.

☐ a. against the law

☐ b. proud

☐ c. amazing

3. When Olivia heard that her aunt had died suddenly, she was so <u>stunned</u> that she almost fainted.

☐ a. shocked

☐ b. relaxed

☐ c. late

4. Sean's knee has a red <u>scar</u> left over from the time he fell onto a jagged piece of glass.

☐ a. a piece of warm clothing worn around the neck

☐ b. a mark on the skin from an old cut or burn

☐ c. a feeling of being frightened

5. At first there was some <u>doubt</u> about which horse won the race. Officials looked at the tape again and finally said that Great News had won.

- ☐ a. feeling of being hungry
- ☐ b. feeling of being sure
- ☐ c. feeling of not being sure

6. Neil said <u>jokingly</u> that he could fly through the air like an eagle.

- ☐ a. in a joking way
- ☐ b. seriously
- ☐ c. angrily

Score 4 points for each correct answer.

_____ **Total Score:** Using Words

E | Author's Approach

Put an X in the box next to the correct answer.

1. What is the author's purpose in writing this article?

- ☐ a. to get readers to consider getting a microchip put in their pets
- ☐ b. to tell the reader that Pooh Bear could fit into a small beach bag
- ☐ c. to describe what Pooh Bear looked like when it was found in Cincinnati, Ohio

2. Choose the statement below that best describes the author's opinion in paragraph 13.

- ☐ a. Pet owners in the United States don't know much about microchips for their pets.
- ☐ b. Pet owners in the United States aren't rich enough to buy microchips for their pets.
- ☐ c. A good collar and tag is just as good as a microchip for pets in the United States.

3. The author tells this story mainly by

- ☐ a. comparing different ideas.
- ☐ b. retelling what happened in time order.
- ☐ c. using his or her imagination.

Score 4 points for each correct answer.

_____ **Total Score:** Author's Approach

F Summarizing and Paraphrasing

Put an X in the box next to the correct answer.

1. Which summary says all the important things?

☐ a. Pooh Bear was a dog that belonged to Bambi Lesne and her family. The family loved their little dog. They carried it around in a small beach bag. In 1996 Pooh Bear disappeared. It was missing for several years.

☐ b. A microchip under your pet's skin may help to bring the pet back to you if it gets lost. You don't need to be afraid that putting the microchip in will hurt your pet. The animal feels only a tiny pinch.

☐ c. Bambi Lesne had a microchip put in her dog. The microchip had a code with Bambi's name. When the dog was found, the microchip led finders back to Bambi. These microchips are used more in other countries than they are in the United States.

2. Which sentence means the same thing as the following sentence? "Pooh Bear was so small she could fit into a small beach bag."

☐ a. Pooh Bear was too small for the tiny beach bag.

☐ b. Even though the beach bag was small, Pooh Bear could fit into it.

☐ c. Pooh Bear found a small beach bag and fit herself into it.

Score 4 points for each correct answer.

_____ **Total Score:** Summarizing and Paraphrasing

G Critical Thinking

Put an X in the box next to the correct answer.

1. Choose the statement below that states a fact.

☐ a. All pet owners who care about their pets should get microchips put in them.

☐ b. Pet microchips went on sale in the 1980s, but 15 years later less than 4 percent of America's dogs and cats had them.

☐ c. Bambi Lesne loves Pooh Bear even more now than she did before she lost the dog.

2. From information in the article, you can predict that

☐ a. if Pooh Bear gets lost again, she will never be found.

☐ b. Dr. Cheryl Devine will tell pet owners to get microchips for their pets.

☐ c. soon Australia will stop making dog owners put microchips in their dogs.

3. Microchips and dog tags are alike because

☐ a. it's a law in the United States for owners to get both for their pets.

☐ b. they can both get lost easily.

☐ c. they are both useful for finding a pet's owner.

4. What was the effect of putting the microchip in Pooh Bear?

☐ a. No one knew where Pooh Bear was for years.

☐ b. After Pooh Bear was found, people called her owner.

☐ c. Dogs in Australia must now have microchips.

5. Which lesson about life does this story teach?

☐ a. You should never give up hope.

☐ b. The wise person always saves money for the future.

☐ c. A picture is worth a thousand words.

Score 4 points for each correct answer.

_____ **Total Score:** Critical Thinking

Enter your score for each activity. Add the scores together. Record your total score on the graph on page 115.

_____ Finding the Main Idea

_____ Recalling Facts

_____ Making Inferences

_____ Using Words

_____ Author's Approach

_____ Summarizing and Paraphrasing

_____ Critical Thinking

_____ **Total Score**

Personal Response

A question I would like answered by Peggy, the woman who found Pooh Bear in Cincinnati, Ohio, is "_____

_____?"

Self-Assessment

One of the things I did best when reading this article was

_____

I believe I did this well because _____

_____

Compare and Contrast

Pick two stories in Unit Two that tell about how science is making our lives better.
Use information from the stories to fill in this chart.

Title	What have scientists learned or invented in each story?	Which people are helped by science in each story?	How are these people helped?

Which of the ideas or inventions would you like to learn more about? Tell why. _____

_____

_____

UNIT THREE

Fly Me to the Moon

At first, the motion of the rocket made Dennis Tito feel a bit sick. But soon he felt better. He then sent a message back to Earth. It said this: "I love space."

2   On April 28, 2001, Tito went where no tourist had ever gone before—to outer space. Of course, every year men and women travel into space. But they do it for research. They are astronauts. They get paid to be in space. But 60-year-old Tito didn't go to do any work. He just went along for the ride.

3   After three days in space, Tito arrived at the International Space Station. This station, called *Alpha*, is 250 miles above Earth. It is the work of many countries. Among them are the United States, Canada, Japan, and many European nations. Tito spent a week here. Then he returned to Earth.

4   Although Tito is an American, he made his trip on a Russian spacecraft. The U.S. space program didn't want him to go. They had many concerns. For one thing,

Pictured here is Dennis Tito, the first tourist in outer space. He paid $20 million to take a ride on a Russian spacecraft.

Alpha was not completely finished in 2001. Parts of it were still being built. The Americans worried that Tito might interfere with the work of the astronauts. He could damage equipment. He could even get hurt.

5   The Russians, on the other hand, were willing to take him. They needed money for their space program. Tito offered to pay them $20 million for the ride. To him, it was worth every cent. As he floated into *Alpha*, he said, "It was a great trip here."

6   Dennis Tito was the first space tourist. A year later, Mark Shuttleworth of South Africa flew to *Alpha* with the Russians. He, too, paid $20 million. Many ordinary people would love to do the same thing. They just don't have the money. After watching Tito and Shuttleworth, some thought, "Isn't that great? When do I get to go?"

7   It may be sooner than they think. Some experts think space tourism could be a big business in 20 or 30 years. They say that spacecraft might fly to space hotels the way jets fly to New York or Paris today. The biggest problem, these scientists say, is cost. The rockets used today cost too much. What is needed is a spacecraft that costs less to launch and that can be used over and over.

8   In 1995 a prize was offered to the first company that could build such a rocket. It was called the X Prize. It was worth $10 million. To claim it, someone had to fly three people into space twice in just two weeks. The same spacecraft had to be used for both trips. On October 4, 2004, someone did it. The spacecraft was called *SpaceShipOne*. Peter Diamandis was the head of the group offering the X Prize. He was happy to pay the $10 million. He knew that most people think space is just for astronauts or the rich. "We want to change that," he said.

9   At least one company is thinking beyond the X Prize. The company is called Space Adventures. It has *really* big plans. It hopes to have "tens of thousands of people in space over the next 10 to 15 years." First, it would send space tourists into orbit around Earth. Later, it would also send tourists to the moon. Space Adventures even hopes to build its own private space stations.

10   Let's imagine that space tourism does become a reality. What would it be like? Tourists in space could stay in hotels just as they do on Earth. These hotels might not be too elegant at first. But as business grows, the space hotels would get bigger and fancier.

11   The guests in a space hotel would float around because they would be weightless. It would seem like there was no gravity. That could be tricky. As a guest in a space hotel, you might find it hard to control your movements. If you moved too fast, you could end up spinning through the air. So you would need to move slowly at first. Soon, though, you'd get the hang of it. Then you could have fun pushing off from one wall with the tips of your fingers and landing on another wall with your feet.

12   People on space vacations might enjoy sports. Just imagine what sports would be like if you were weightless. In space basketball, it would not matter how tall or short you were. Everyone could float through the air to dunk the ball. Your weight would not matter either. Everyone would weigh exactly the same—zero.

13   The rules of golf would have to change. In space, a golf ball would not drop into the hole. And what about water sports? In space, water would float around in blobs. You might try a new form of dodge ball. Instead of a ball, players could toss water blobs at each other.

14   There is one more difference that space tourists would enjoy. The views would be incredible. From space, you could see whole continents. You could see storms moving across the oceans. And you could see spaceships bringing new guests to your hotel.

15   Let's just hope that when space tourism becomes a reality, the guests aren't still paying $20 million a seat! 🎗

A | Finding the Main Idea

One statement below tells the main idea of the article. One statement is too general, or too broad. The other statement explains only part of the article; it is too narrow. Label the statements using the following key:

M—Main Idea   B—Too Broad   N—Too Narrow

_____ 1. For many people, travel is one of the great joys in life. Until now, people have been limited to traveling to places on Earth. In the future, people might travel to other places.

_____ 2. In 2001 Dennis Tito paid the Russians $20 million to take him to the International Space Station, about 250 miles above Earth. People say that he was the first space tourist.

_____ 3. A few rich people such as Dennis Tito and Mark Shuttleworth have been able to travel in space just for fun. In the future, ordinary people may be able to do that too.

Score 4 points for each correct answer.

_____ **Total Score:** Finding the Main Idea

B | Recalling Facts

How well do you remember the facts in the article? Put an X in the box next to the answer that correctly completes each statement.

1. When Dennis Tito traveled to the space station, he was

☐ a. 25 years old.
☐ b. 42 years old.
☐ c. 60 years old.

2. Mark Shuttleworth came from

☐ a. the United States.
☐ b. South Africa.
☐ c. Europe.

3. Someone won the X Prize using a spacecraft called

☐ a. *Diamandis.*
☐ b. *SpaceShipOne.*
☐ c. *Alpha.*

4. People traveling in space would

☐ a. get old more quickly than they would on Earth.
☐ b. be heavier than they are on Earth.
☐ c. feel no gravity and float around easily.

Score 4 points for each correct answer.

_____ **Total Score:** Recalling Facts

C | Making Inferences

When you draw a conclusion that is not directly stated in the text, you are making an inference. Put an X in the box next to the statement that is a correct inference.

1.

☐ a. Dennis Tito and Mark Shuttleworth are men who don't mind taking chances.

☐ b. The Russians were sure that Dennis Tito would not hurt himself or anyone else on the trip to the space shuttle.

☐ c. Dennis Tito probably did interfere with the astronauts' work when he got to the space station.

2.

☐ a. Space Adventures probably wants to make it free to travel in space.

☐ b. In space, the way certain sports are played would change.

☐ c. In the future, no one will be happy staying at the hotels in space because they won't be fancy enough.

Score 4 points for each correct answer.

_____ **Total Score:** Making Inferences

D | Using Words

Put an X in the box next to the definition below that is closest in meaning to the underlined word.

1. If you stay, you will <u>interfere</u> with my work. So if you want to help, please leave me alone.

☐ a. make easier

☐ b. explain

☐ c. get in the way

2. This city encourages <u>tourism</u> by building fancy hotels and good restaurants for people on vacation.

☐ a. staying at home

☐ b. traveling for pleasure

☐ c. hard work

3. Carol's dream of winning first prize for her quilts became a <u>reality</u> when she was given the blue ribbon at the state fair.

☐ a. something that will never happen

☐ b. something that is imagined

☐ c. a real thing

4. Everyone admired the lovely princess, who wore an <u>elegant</u> lace gown and long white gloves.

☐ a. dirty

☐ b. ugly

☐ c. fancy

5. Without <u>gravity</u>, we would all be floating in space.

☐ a. the force that pulls things toward big objects
☐ b. the condition of being important
☐ c. the state of having no weight

6. The artist threw colorful <u>blobs</u> of paint on a large sheet of paper and called it art.

☐ a. soft or wet lumps
☐ b. invisible gases
☐ c. terrible sounds

Score 4 points for each correct answer.

_____ **Total Score:** Using Words

E Author's Approach

Put an X in the box next to the correct answer.

1. The author uses the first sentence of the article to

☐ a. tell how Dennis Tito felt when he traveled into space.
☐ b. explain why Dennis Tito wanted to travel into space.
☐ c. describe the rocket on which Dennis Tito traveled into space.

2. Choose the statement below that is the weakest argument for traveling in space.

☐ a. Space travel could be dangerous.
☐ b. Space travel is exciting.
☐ c. In space, you would have experiences you could not have on Earth.

3. The author probably wrote this article in order to

☐ a. explain why the United States didn't want Dennis Tito to go to the space station.
☐ b. get readers ready to travel to outer space.
☐ c. tell the reader about something exciting that scientists are working on.

Score 4 points for each correct answer.

_____ **Total Score:** Author's Approach

F | Summarizing and Paraphrasing

Put an X in the box next to the correct answer.

1. Which summary says all the important things about the article?

☐ a. Dennis Tito and Mark Shuttleworth were not paid to be astronauts, but they have traveled in space. They both paid $20 million to go to the space station *Alpha*. Scientists and others are working on ways for other people to travel in space too. On a trip to space, people could do and see things they could not do on Earth.

☐ b. In space, people would be weightless. Sports would be different. How tall or heavy a player is wouldn't matter. Everyone would float around. Everyone would weigh zero pounds.

☐ c. The International Space Station *Alpha* is about 250 miles above Earth. Many countries have worked on it. When Dennis Tito wanted to go there, he had to pay the Russians $20 million. Tito spent a week there in 2001.

2. Which sentence means the same thing as the following sentence? "Soon, though, you'd get the hang of it."

☐ a. In a short time, you would want to hang it up.

☐ b. After a little while, you would get good at it.

☐ c. Very soon, you would want to leave.

Score 4 points for each correct answer.

_____ **Total Score:** Summarizing and Paraphrasing

G | Critical Thinking

Put an X in the box next to the correct answer.

1. Choose the statement below that states an opinion.

☐ a. In 2002 Mark Shuttleworth paid $20 million to travel in space.

☐ b. The winner of the X Prize got $10 million for flying one spacecraft into space twice in two weeks.

☐ c. It would be exciting and fun to travel to the space station.

2. From information in the article, you can predict that

☐ a. in the future, ordinary people will be able travel in space.

☐ b. in the future, only rich people will travel in space.

☐ c. in the future, space travel will become too dangerous for anyone.

3. Dennis Tito and Mark Shuttleworth are different because

☐ a. only Tito went to the space station *Alpha*.

☐ b. only Tito is an American.

☐ c. only Shuttleworth is rich.

4. The U.S. space program didn't want to take Dennis Tito to the space station. What was the cause of the Americans' concerns?

☐ a. They were worried that Tito might get sick or even die in space.

☐ b. They were afraid that Tito might steal secrets about the space shuttle and sell it to another country.

☐ c. They were afraid that Tito might bother the astronauts, damage equipment, or get hurt.

5. In which paragraph did you find the information or details to answer question 4?

☐ a. paragraph 4

☐ b. paragraph 5

☐ c. paragraph 6

Score 4 points for each correct answer.

_____ **Total Score:** Critical Thinking

Enter your score for each activity. Add the scores together. Record your total score on the graph on page 115.

_____ Finding the Main Idea

_____ Recalling Facts

_____ Making Inferences

_____ Using Words

_____ Author's Approach

_____ Summarizing and Paraphrasing

_____ Critical Thinking

_____ **Total Score**

Personal Response

I agree with the author because _____

_____

_____

Self-Assessment

I can't really understand how _____

_____

Can Electricity Make You Sick?

Pictured are large electric power lines that send electricity. Some people think they are allergic to electricity.

Joan Stock can't go through the checkout line in a grocery store. She can't get near a computer. She can't even ride in a new car. She is not afraid of these things. She is allergic to them. Or at least she is allergic to the microchips contained in them.

2 When Stock does get near a microchip, she gets a blinding headache. According to her, it is "very frightening." The pain is "completely out of my control."

3 Stock's doctors say her headaches are caused by the signals coming from microchips. Most people are not bothered by these electrical waves. Most people are not bothered by electricity in any form. Indeed, electricity is all around us. And it has been since the beginning of time. The lightning that comes in a storm is one example. The human body has its own electrical system. The brain sends electrical messages to the rest of the body.

4 These days, though, electrical waves come from a variety of new sources. Power lines send them out. So do car engines. TVs produce them. Radios do too. In fact, all things that plug in, use batteries, or contain microchips send out these waves. In Joan Stock's case, this is a big problem. The electrical waves from microchips interrupt the electrical waves of her brain. That causes intense headaches.

5 Stock is happy to know what the problem is. But her life will never be the same again. "Everything has computer chips in it these days," she says. She finds herself very limited in terms of "what I can do and where I can go."

6 Stock is not the only one who is allergic to electricity. Christine Moody is too. Moody, who lives in England, can't wear a watch. She can't get near phone lines. She feels pain when she crosses a street that has underground power lines. "Life is difficult," she says. She just tries to "get through a day at a time."

7 In Sweden, Per Segerbäck does the same thing. Like Stock and Moody, he has to be very careful. He says that his skin "hurts when I am exposed to electricity." If he stays near electrical sources too long, his skin turns red. Patches of his skin actually get burned. He also becomes less energetic. "I only want to lie down and sleep," he says.

8 Other people report other problems. Some get dizzy. They may black out. Their muscles ache. They may have trouble seeing. Often they feel sick to their stomachs.

9 Arthur Firstenberg says his whole body tingles and shakes. "Imagine sticking your hand in a light socket," he says. That's what it feels like every time he passes something that is plugged in.

10   Don Kaput of California had a particularly bad case. He heard ringing in his ears. His heart beat wildly, and he couldn't eat. His knees swelled. He got sick whenever he went near the TV. Going to bed brought no relief. His water bed was heated with electricity.

11   As time passed, Kaput's health got worse and worse.

12   "He was close to death," says his wife, Melissa.

13   In 2001 the family finally figured out what was wrong with him. They knew what they had to do. They left their home and moved out into the wilderness. There, far from all forms of electricity, Don Kaput got better. By 2003 his daughter Danielle could say, "I think he's back to his old self."

14   These cases sound clear-cut. But not all doctors are convinced. Some do not think electricity is to blame. They point to other things. Rand Malone is an expert on the subject. He says it's likely that people are actually allergic to chemicals or smells instead of electricity. Other experts think that people like Don Kaput and Joan Stock are just making up their problems.

15   Dr. David Dowson takes a different stand. He says that being allergic to electricity is real. It's just rare. It is so rare, in fact, that some folks have not heard of it. These folks think the problem is all a joke. They spread the idea that the disease is all in someone's head. But, says Dr. Dowson, "It is certainly not."

16   Dr. Gunnar Heusar agrees with Dowson. Heusar has treated more than 20 people who are allergic to electricity. He is sure that it is "a real medical disease." He said those who have it "are in urgent need of relief."

17   So who is right? Are some people really allergic to electricity? Or is something else causing their problems? Perhaps someday that question can be answered once and for all. Doctors on both sides agree that more studies would help. There is a lot we don't know about how electricity affects the body. In the meantime, people like Don Kaput and Joan Stock have no doubt. They are sure that electricity is to blame. They know some people don't believe it. But they don't care. Says Kaput, "I've accepted what has happened to me, whether you believe it or not."

A | Finding the Main Idea

One statement below tells the main idea of the article. One statement is too general, or too broad. The other statement explains only part of the article; it is too narrow. Label the statements using the following key:

M—Main Idea   **B—Too Broad**   **N—Too Narrow**

_____ 1. Don Kaput of California had a bad allergy to electrical waves. He was getting sicker and sicker. Finally, he and his family moved to the wilderness where there are fewer electrical waves. He got much better.

_____ 2. Some people believe they are allergic to electricity. They say that electrical waves from microchips and other sources are making them sick. While some experts agree that these people are allergic to electrical waves, others are not so sure.

_____ 3. Electricity is a force that has always been around us. In recent years, many new sources have been sending out electrical waves. It is possible that the waves are having effects that no one could have imagined.

Score 4 points for each correct answer.

_____ **Total Score:** Finding the Main Idea

B | Recalling Facts

How well do you remember the facts in the article? Put an X in the box next to the answer that correctly completes each statement.

1. Joan Stock's doctors believe that signals from microchips are
   - ☐ a. making her skin turn red.
   - ☐ b. making her go blind.
   - ☐ c. giving her bad headaches.

2. All of these send out electrical waves <u>except</u>
   - ☐ a. radios.
   - ☐ b. scissors.
   - ☐ c. computers.

3. Rand Malone believes that people who think they are allergic to electricity are really allergic to
   - ☐ a. chemicals.
   - ☐ b. sunlight.
   - ☐ c. green plants.

4. Dr. David Dowson says that being allergic to electricity is
   - ☐ a. just a joke.
   - ☐ b. not possible.
   - ☐ c. real.

Score 4 points for each correct answer.

_____ **Total Score:** Recalling Facts

C Making Inferences

When you draw a conclusion that is not directly stated in the text, you are making an inference. Put an X in the box next to the statement that is a correct inference.

1.

☐ a. Joan Stock probably rides in a car that is several years old.

☐ b. Joan Stock enjoys going grocery shopping.

☐ c. Joan Stock's kitchen is probably filled with the latest cooking and baking machines.

2.

☐ a. There are no electrical waves at all in the wilderness where Don Kaput and his family moved.

☐ b. Guessing that patients are allergic to electricity is the first way most doctors try to explain headaches.

☐ c. The parts of our bodies are connected. When one part has a problem, other parts are affected.

Score 4 points for each correct answer.

_____ **Total Score:** Making Inferences

D Using Words

Put an X in the box next to the definition below that is closest in meaning to the underlined word.

1. Because Gene is <u>allergic</u> to animal fur, he keeps tissues in his pocket when he goes to the pet shop.

☐ a. suffering from a condition that makes people afraid to leave their own homes

☐ b. suffering from a condition that makes people sneeze, cough, or feel sick when they touch or eat certain things

☐ c. suffering from a condition that makes people feel sad all the time

2. The lightning storm knocked out our house's <u>electrical</u> system. For days we had to use candles to see at night.

☐ a. having to do with houses

☐ b. having to do with storms

☐ c. having to do with electricity

3. This store carries a <u>variety</u> of batteries for items such as flashlights, cameras, and watches.

☐ a. a group of things that are exactly the same

☐ b. the cost of an item

☐ c. a number of different types

4. Eli has an <u>intense</u> dislike of green peppers and absolutely refuses to eat them.

☐ a. very strong

☐ b. very weak

☐ c. very surprising

5. I feel most <u>energetic</u> in the morning. At that time of day, I am ready for any job, no matter how hard it may be.

☐ a. hungry
☐ b. tired
☐ c. lively

6. Pull the plug from the wall before you screw the light bulb into the <u>socket</u>.

☐ a. a book with instructions for fixing things around the house
☐ b. something hollow that something else fits into
☐ c. a kind of pipe through which water runs

Score 4 points for each correct answer.

_____ **Total Score:** Using Words

E | Author's Approach

Put an X in the box next to the correct answer.

1. The main purpose of the first paragraph is to

☐ a. describe what Joan Stock does every day.
☐ b. tell exactly what happens to Joan Stock when she comes near electricity.
☐ c. tell how being allergic to electricity has limited Joan Stock's life.

2. Choose the statement below that best explains how the author deals with the opposite point of view.

☐ a. The author says that Joan Stock has complained that her pain is out of control.
☐ b. The author tells what both kinds of experts say—those who believe it is possible to be allergic to electricity and those who are not sure.
☐ c. The author describes the problems that several people have had. The author explains that they all blame these problems on being allergic to electricity.

3. The author tells this story mainly by

☐ a. telling what different people believe about the problem.
☐ b. telling about events in the order they happened.
☐ c. using his or her imagination to guess how electricity is causing problems.

Score 4 points for each correct answer.

_____ **Total Score:** Author's Approach

F Summarizing and Paraphrasing

Put an X in the box next to the correct answer.

1. Which summary says all the important things?

☐ a. Electricity is all around us. It is found in natural events such as lightning storms. And it is even found within our own bodies. In fact, the brain is always sending out electrical signals to parts of the body.

☐ b. The use of electricity is constantly growing. Some people say that they are allergic to electrical waves. Many experts believe these people face a real problem. Other experts think that electricity is not to blame. Further research on the subject is needed.

☐ c. Joan Stock, Christine Moody, Per Segerbäck, Arthur Firstenberg, and Don Kaput have a common problem. All of them believe that they are allergic to electricity. They suffer from headaches, pains, burned skin, lowered energy, and body shakes.

2. Which sentence means the same thing as the following sentence? "Stock is not the only one who is allergic to electricity."

☐ a. Electricity makes no one but Stock sick.

☐ b. Stock is unhappy that no one else seems to be allergic to electricity but her.

☐ c. Other people besides Stock are allergic to electricity.

Score 4 points for each correct answer.

_____ **Total Score:** Summarizing and Paraphrasing

G Critical Thinking

Put an X in the box next to the correct answer.

1. Choose the statement below that states a fact.

☐ a. The world would be a better place without electricity.

☐ b. People should stop making machines that send out electrical waves.

☐ c. The brain sends electrical messages to the rest of the body.

2. Joan Stock and Per Segerbäck are alike because

☐ a. both live in England.

☐ b. both get blinding headaches from electricity.

☐ c. both believe they are allergic to electricity.

3. What was the effect of Don Kaput's move to the wilderness?

☐ a. His whole body started to tingle and shake.

☐ b. He started feeling much better.

☐ c. His heart started to beat wildly, and he could not eat.

4. Which paragraphs provide information that supports your answer to question 3?

☐ a. paragraphs 1 to 3

☐ b. paragraphs 6 and 7

☐ c. paragraphs 10 to 13

5. If you were a doctor, how could you use the information in the article to treat patients who complained of bad headaches or muscle pains?

☐ a. I would tell them their problems were all in their heads.

☐ b. I would check to see whether they were allergic to electricity.

☐ c. I would tell them to stop complaining so much because nothing could be done for them.

Score 4 points for each correct answer.

_____ **Total Score:** Critical Thinking

Enter your score for each activity. Add the scores together. Record your total score on the graph on page 115.

_____ Finding the Main Idea

_____ Recalling Facts

_____ Making Inferences

_____ Using Words

_____ Author's Approach

_____ Summarizing and Paraphrasing

_____ Critical Thinking

_____ **Total Score**

Personal Response

I can't believe _____

_____

Self-Assessment

From reading this article, I have learned _____

_____

High-Tech Hikers

It was just supposed to be a day trip. Chris Stricker and Eddy Millers wanted to take pictures of the beautiful Pennsylvania mountains. They set out early on October 7, 2000. To get the best view, they climbed up a cliff on top of Mount Minsi. But there they ran into trouble. Stricker and Millers stayed too long at the top. As it grew dark, they realized that it was too dangerous to climb down. But snow was expected that night. And the two men were not dressed in warm clothes.

2 They were stuck. But luckily, they had a cell phone. They called the state police, who alerted park officials. Stricker and Millers built a campfire so they could be seen more easily. At 1 A.M., rescuers arrived and brought the two men off the mountain. "This was a good rescue," said park official Ed Whitaker. "Nobody was hurt, and the guys are safe. They were wise to call for help."

3 Stricker and Millers owed their lives to the people who came for them. But they also owed their lives to

---

Hikers need to use their skills in the mountains. High-tech tools also come in handy when hikers get into trouble.

their cell phone. These days, more and more hikers are carrying such high-tech tools to keep them safe.

4 One of these tools is a Global Positioning System, or GPS. With this, you carry a tiny receiver. It lets you know where you are. The receiver sends a signal into space. Satellites in orbit over Earth pick up the signal. The satellites figure out how far north or south you are. They also figure out how far east or west you are. Then they send back a signal telling you your position to within 50 feet.

5 Don Shelby was carrying a GPS receiver in the summer of 2000. That turned out to be a good thing. Shelby and some friends headed out on a long trip. They rode their horses up into the mountains of Montana. Shelby had done plenty of hiking and riding before. He had climbed mountains everywhere from Africa to South America. So he knew what he was doing. Still, he had brought along a GPS receiver just in case.

6 The group was 26 miles out into the wilderness when trouble arose. Shelby's horse acted up. It suddenly reared back. As it did so, its head struck Shelby's head. The blow knocked Shelby unconscious. It broke a bone in his shoulder and cracked his skull. When he woke up, he was in so much pain that he couldn't move.

7   That's when Shelby's GPS receiver came in very handy. Shelby's friends took it out and noted their location. Then one of them rode off to get help. Thanks to the GPS, the friend could tell the search party exactly where Shelby was. They then used a helicopter to pick Shelby up.

8   In July 2003, another new instrument went on sale. It had been around for a long time. Sailors and pilots had used it for 20 years. But now other people could buy one too. It is called a personal locator beacon, or PLB. Like the GPS, it uses satellites. But there is a difference. A GPS tells *you* where you are. A PLB tells the people searching for you where you are. You don't have to send for help. If you get in trouble, you simply push a button. That sends out a signal letting others know you're in trouble. Thanks to the PLB, they can tell exactly where you are. Within a minute, they can be making plans to rescue you.

9   In November 2003, Carl Skalak learned how well a PLB can work. He was spending a week in his cabin in the Adirondack Mountains. The weather turned bad. Skalak stuck it out for several days of high winds and heavy rain. Then the temperature dropped, and the rain turned to snow. About 20 inches fell. There was no way this 55-year-old man could walk out. Skalak knew his life was in danger, so he pushed the button on his PLB. That was all it took. Soon after the signal went out, a rescue party rushed to get him. "The system worked like a gem," said one official. Without his PLB, Skalak might well have died.

10 High-tech tools can be great, but people need to be careful. They must use the tools correctly. If you send a PLB signal when there is no danger, you'll be in big trouble. You could spend six years in jail and owe a $250,000 fine.

11 There is another danger too. People may start to count on these tools too much. They could lose skills such as reading a map or using a compass. What would happen to them if their cell phone could not pick up a signal? What would happen if their PLB or GPS receiver fell into a lake? Cliff Jacobson, who works as a guide, owns a GPS receiver. He claims it has saved his life more than once. Even so, he worries that his outdoor skills are fading. Jacobson says high-tech tools have dulled our ability "to sniff our way through a fog."

12 Ann Bancroft, who has walked across Antarctica, agrees. "There's a great danger in it," she says. People get into trouble "because they think help is only a telephone call away."

13 Still, the technology is here to stay. And on balance, that's probably a good thing. Even Ann Bancroft says, "I know there are countless stories where it has saved people's lives."

A | Finding the Main Idea

One statement below tells the main idea of the article. One statement is too general, or too broad. The other statement explains only part of the article; it is too narrow. Label the statements using the following key:

M—Main Idea   B—Too Broad   N—Too Narrow

_____ 1. People who like to go out into the wilderness are now using new tools such as cell phones, GPS receivers, and PLBs. These new tools are making their wilderness experience safer. However, there is a chance that people will start depending on the tools too much.

_____ 2. Technology is changing our lives every day. Using technology, we are finding that things that we thought were impossible only a few years ago can be done easily. New inventions help us even when we are having fun.

_____ 3. The Global Positioning System, or GPS, lets you know where you are on the face of Earth. Its receiver sends a signal into space. The signal is picked up by satellites. They figure out where you are and send back a signal that gives you that information.

> Score 4 points for each correct answer.
>
> _____ **Total Score:** Finding the Main Idea

B | Recalling Facts

How well do you remember the facts in the article? Put an X in the box next to the answer that correctly completes each statement.

1. When Stricker and Millers wanted to find someone to help them get down Mount Minsi, they used

   ☐ a. a cell phone to call for help.
   ☐ b. a GPS receiver to find out where they were.
   ☐ c. a PLB to tell others where they were.

2. Don Shelby got into trouble when

   ☐ a. he got lost in the mountains of Montana.
   ☐ b. his horse reared back and knocked him unconscious.
   ☐ c. his GPS receiver fell into a lake and didn't work anymore.

3. Hikers should use a Personal Locator Beacon, or PLB, when they

   ☐ a. want to let someone know where they are.
   ☐ b. are lonely and feel like talking to a friend.
   ☐ c. want to find out how to get back home.

4. According to the article, if you use a PLB when you are not in danger, you could be punished with

   ☐ a. jail for six months and a $250 fine.
   ☐ b. jail for two years and a $10,000 fine.
   ☐ c. jail for six years and a $250,000 fine.

> Score 4 points for each correct answer.
>
> _____ **Total Score:** Recalling Facts

C Making Inferences

When you draw a conclusion that is not directly stated in the text, you are making an inference. Put an X in the box next to the statement that is a correct inference.

1.

☐ a. Don Shelby did not prepare for his trip to the mountains of Montana well enough.

☐ b. Park official Ed Whitaker gets upset when people call for help instead of taking care of themselves in the wilderness.

☐ c. It is easier to get a helicopter into a wild area than it is to land a plane there.

2.

☐ a. For someone who is in the wilderness and not able to move, having a PLB is more useful than having a GPS.

☐ b. If there were no satellites going around Earth, a GPS would still work fine.

☐ c. Almost everyone who goes on a hike takes along either a GPS receiver or a PLB.

Score 4 points for each correct answer.

_____ **Total Score:** Making Inferences

D Using Words

Put an X in the box next to the definition below that is closest in meaning to the underlined word.

1. As soon as his underline{receiver} got the signal from space, the hiker knew where he was.

☐ a. a tool that allows users to make phone calls
☐ b. a tool that gives users an electric shock
☐ c. a tool that receives signals

2. On clear nights, you may be able to spot satellites moving across the sky.

☐ a. small, furry animals that live in the high branches of trees
☐ b. stories about imaginary people, places, or things
☐ c. objects that travel around Earth or other bodies in space

3. After Bonnie fell off the swing, she was unconscious for a moment. Then she woke up and started to cry.

☐ a. unaware of what is going on around one
☐ b. angry about things that are happening around one
☐ c. interested in everything happening

4. The location of the stalled car is the corner of Maple Street and Broadway Avenue.

☐ a. owner's name and age
☐ b. the place where something is
☐ c. license number

5. The <u>gem</u> for June is the pearl.

  ☐ a. a special plant, such as a large oak tree
  ☐ b. something of great value, like a beautiful stone
  ☐ c. something that no one wants, such as bad luck

6. Doctors use the latest <u>technology</u>, including special machines and tools, to treat their patients.

  ☐ a. medicine
  ☐ b. diseases that can pass from person to person
  ☐ c. the use of scientific knowledge for particular goals

Score 4 points for each correct answer.

_____ **Total Score:** Using Words

E | Author's Approach

Put an X in the box next to the correct answer.

1. The main purpose of the first paragraph is to

  ☐ a. tell how a cell phone saved the lives of two men.
  ☐ b. describe the mountains of Pennsylvania.
  ☐ c. tell about the problem Stricker and Millers faced.

2. What is the author's purpose in writing this article?

  ☐ a. to make the reader feel nervous about hiking
  ☐ b. to tell the reader about new tools that can save lives
  ☐ c. to urge readers to do without the latest tools

3. From the statements below, choose the one that you believe the author would agree with.

  ☐ a. People had more fun before they had tools such as cell phones and GPS receivers.
  ☐ b. Technology is making the wilderness less dangerous for people.
  ☐ c. Only hikers with no experience would bother to take a GPS receiver with them on a hike.

Score 4 points for each correct answer.

_____ **Total Score:** Author's Approach

F | Summarizing and Paraphrasing

Put an X in the box next to the correct answer.

1. Which summary says all the important things?

☐ a. It is important for hikers to know how to read a map and use a compass. When trouble hits, they cannot always count on the latest tools to keep in touch with people or to let searchers know where they are.

☐ b. New tools such as cell phones, GPS receivers, and PLBs are changing the way hikers and other lovers of the outdoors operate. These tools make it possible for hikers to keep in touch, to find out where they are, and to signal when they need help. They work so well that people may begin to count on them too much.

☐ c. A PLB can come in handy. That is what Carl Skalak learned. He was spending some time in his cabin when it began to snow. That was when Skalak used a PLB to signal that he was in trouble.

2. Which sentence means the same thing as the following sentence? "'The system worked like a gem,' said one official."

☐ a. One official said that the system could be improved.

☐ b. One official reported that the system worked well.

☐ c. According to one official, the system was as hard as a stone.

Score 4 points for each correct answer.

_____ **Total Score:** Summarizing and Paraphrasing

G | Critical Thinking

Put an X in the box next to the correct answer.

1. Choose the statement below that states a fact.

☐ a. Hiking is more fun when you know you are safe.

☐ b. Every hiker should carry a PLB.

☐ c. PLBs went on sale in July 2003.

2. From information in the article, you can predict that

☐ a. hikers will use tools such as cell phones, GPS receivers, and PLBs even more in the future.

☐ b. Cliff Jacobson, a guide, will decide to never use his GPS receiver again.

☐ c. in the future, there will be no punishment for using a PLB even when a person is not facing danger.

3. GPS and PLB are different because

☐ a. only the GPS uses satellites to do its job.

☐ b. only the PLB tells other people where you are.

☐ c. only the GPS is useful when you are in trouble.

4. Stricker and Millers built a campfire while they were waiting for help. What was the cause of their action?

☐ a. They hoped that anyone looking for them would see the fire and then find them.

☐ b. They needed to dry their clothes by the fire.

☐ c. They were bored and needed something to do to keep themselves entertained.

5. In which paragraph did you find the information or details to answer question 4?

☐ a. paragraph 3

☐ b. paragraph 1

☐ c. paragraph 2

Score 4 points for each correct answer.

_____ **Total Score:** Critical Thinking

Enter your score for each activity. Add the scores together. Record your total score on the graph on page 115.

_____ Finding the Main Idea

_____ Recalling Facts

_____ Making Inferences

_____ Using Words

_____ Author's Approach

_____ Summarizing and Paraphrasing

_____ Critical Thinking

_____ **Total Score**

Personal Response

Describe a time when you were on a hike or a trip and needed help. _____

_____

Self-Assessment

When reading the article, I was having trouble with

_____

_____

Separate Lives

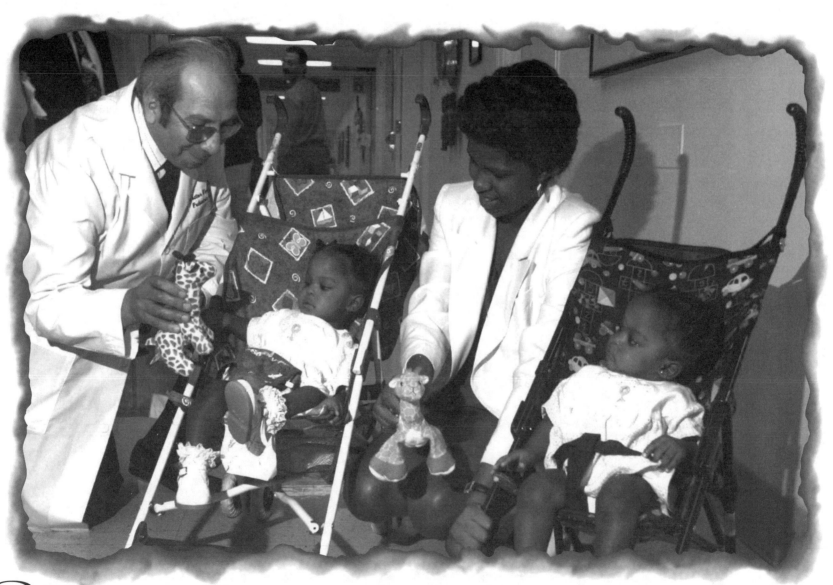

Dr. Cindy Howard happened to be in the right place at the right time. Howard worked at the University of Maryland Medical Center. But in the fall of 2001, she was visiting a hospital in Uganda in eastern Africa. She was there when a set of newborn twins was brought in. Everyone was talking about these baby girls. Their African names meant "most beautiful" and "most special." And the girls were both of these things. But they were also in danger. If doctors could not help them, they would not live to grow up.

2 The babies were conjoined twins. That meant their bodies were joined together. Each girl had her own head, arms, and legs. Each also had most of her own organs. But they were joined together from their chests to just above their hips.

3 Conjoined twins are very rare. In the whole world, only about 200 sets are born each year. They are formed early in a mother's pregnancy. They are always identical twins. That means they come from a single egg that has split in two. But in the case of conjoined twins, the split is incomplete. So the two babies share certain body parts.

4 About half of all conjoined twins die before birth. Many more die within the first 24 hours. A few get lucky. They don't share too many body parts. So they have a chance at life. Some of these twins stay connected for their whole lives. Others have operations to be separated. When the little Ugandan girls were brought to the hospital, they seemed healthy. But the one called Christine was growing more quickly than her sister, Loice [lo-EES]. That's because some of Loice's blood was flowing into Christine's body. In time, the difference in their size and weight would cause problems. These problems would lead to their death.

5 The doctors in Uganda knew the girls had to be separated. It was the only way to save them. But these doctors could not do it. They did not have the training. They did not have the equipment. So they turned to Dr. Howard. Would her hospital back in Maryland be willing to help?

6 The answer was yes. The hospital was more than willing to help. The girls' parents, Gordon and Margret Onzigas, were poor farmers. They had no money. So the hospital agreed to do the operation for free.

Pictured here are formerly conjoined twins. These twins were separated and are now leading happy separate lives.

A medical team of 35 people would be needed to do it. Every team member volunteered his or her services. None of them wanted a dime. All they wanted was to help these little girls live.

7   Early in 2002, Christine and Loice arrived in Maryland with their parents. Gordon and Margret were scared. Doctors told them there was a 20 percent chance the babies would die during the operation. But without it, the Onzigas could only go back to their village and wait for their daughters to die. So they told the doctors to go ahead.

8   The medical team worked hard to get ready. They tried to think of everything that could go wrong. They even held a practice run. They used two dolls that had been sewn together. Pretending that these dolls were Loice and Christine, the doctors planned every move they would need to make.

9   On April 19, it was time for the real thing. The doctors spent six hours getting the twins ready. As they put six-month-old Christine and Loice to sleep, they kept an eye on both heart rates. Then the doctors began the process of separating the girls. First, the girls' liver had to be separated. So did many blood vessels. Christine and Loice had shared part of their rib cage, so that had to be divided. At last doctors got to the girls' hearts. There they discovered a problem. They had thought the hearts were separate. That was how things had looked in every test they had run. But now they saw that this was not really the case.

10   Dr. Marcelo Cardarelli said, "It was only after we got inside that we learned that the girls shared a large vein in the heart."

11   No one knew what would happen when this vein was cut. Could the two hearts work separately? Before doctors could go any further, they had to find out. Team members held their breath as they pinched off the vein. "Those two little hearts continued beating as if it was their inherent right," said Dr. Bartley Griffith.

12   With that huge piece of good news, doctors continued. At last, after 12 hours, they finished, and Christine and Loice were still asleep. For the first time in their lives, they could be put in separate cribs. When their mother saw them, she was filled with joy. "I wanted to cry," she said.

13   "Today my wife and I are very happy parents to see both our daughters alive and separate," said Gordon.

14   It took months for the girls to get well enough and strong enough to go home. But soon after the girls' first birthday, Gordon and Margret took them back home to their small Ugandan village. Dr. Cindy Howard made the trip with them. Thanks to her and dozens of others at the University of Maryland hospital, Christine and Loice Onzigas could now lead long, healthy lives.

A | Finding the Main Idea

One statement below tells the main idea of the article. One statement is too general, or too broad. The other statement explains only part of the article; it is too narrow. Label the statements using the following key:

M—Main Idea   **B—Too Broad**   **N—Too Narrow**

_____ 1. In 2002 doctors at the University of Maryland hospital separated twin girls who had been born joined from the chests to the hips. They did the difficult operation for free. The girls returned to their home in Uganda several months later.

_____ 2. To get ready for the operation to separate Christine and Loice Onzigas, the staff at the University of Maryland hospital practiced what they would do. They pretended that two dolls sewed together were the girls. Using the dolls, they planned each move they would make.

_____ 3. People, especially people who don't have enough money, often need help. It is good to know that there are kind people in the world who are willing to give their time and skills in order to help those in need.

Score 4 points for each correct answer.

_____ **Total Score:** Finding the Main Idea

B | Recalling Facts

How well do you remember the facts in the article? Put an X in the box next to the answer that correctly completes each statement.

1. Conjoined twins
☐ a. come from two eggs that get stuck together.
☐ b. always die within a year.
☐ c. share body parts.

2. The Onzigas twins' parents were
☐ a. doctors.
☐ b. farmers.
☐ c. scientists.

3. During the operation, doctors were surprised to find out that
☐ a. the girls shared a large vein in their hearts.
☐ b. the twins shared a brain.
☐ c. the twins' liver had to be divided.

4. The operation lasted
☐ a. two hours.
☐ b. six hours.
☐ c. 12 hours.

Score 4 points for each correct answer.

_____ **Total Score:** Recalling Facts

C | Making Inferences

When you draw a conclusion that is not directly stated in the text, you are making an inference. Put an X in the box next to the statement that is a correct inference.

1.

☐ a. Conjoined twins look exactly the same throughout their lives.

☐ b. Doctors know everything they will find inside someone's body even before they begin an operation.

☐ c. If Dr. Howard hadn't been in Uganda when the twins were born, she probably would not have helped them.

2.

☐ a. A person can live with only half a liver.

☐ b. A person needs only half a heart to live.

☐ c. A person can't live without a whole rib cage.

Score 4 points for each correct answer.

_____ **Total Score:** Making Inferences

D | Using Words

Put an X in the box next to the definition below that is closest in meaning to the underlined word.

1. Most <u>newborn</u> babies weigh less than 10 pounds.

☐ a. imaginary

☐ b. smiling

☐ c. just born

2. A woman must be careful about what she eats during her <u>pregnancy</u>. What she eats can affect her baby.

☐ a. the condition of having a disease

☐ b. the state of having a baby growing inside the body

☐ c. the state of having a young child to care for

3. At first I thought that these leaves were <u>identical</u>, but now I see some differences between them.

☐ a. exactly the same

☐ b. unlike one another

☐ c. beautiful

4. The symphony is <u>incomplete</u> because the composer died before she could get it done.

☐ a. perfect

☐ b. famous

☐ c. not finished

5. You would have lost even more blood if you had cut a larger <u>vein</u>.

☐ a. one of the bones in the hand
☐ b. a blood vessel
☐ c. an electric cord

6. From the moment they are born, babies have an <u>inherent</u> fear of falling.

☐ a. built in
☐ b. practiced
☐ c. learned

Score 4 points for each correct answer.

_____ **Total Score:** Using Words

E Author's Approach

Put an X in the box next to the correct answer.

1. The main purpose of the first paragraph is to

☐ a. to explain how Dr. Cindy Howard heard about the conjoined twins.
☐ b. to show how rare it is that some twins are born joined together.
☐ c. to tell the reader that Dr. Cindy Howard worked at the University of Maryland Medical Center.

2. What is the author's purpose in writing this article?

☐ a. to compare hospitals in Uganda and the United States
☐ b. to show how science helped change the lives of a set of conjoined twins
☐ c. to explain how conjoined twins are formed

3. Choose the statement below that best describes the author's opinion in paragraph 6.

☐ a. The Onzigas family should have paid the doctors at the University of Maryland hospital.
☐ b. Members of the hospital staff seemed upset that they wouldn't get paid for doing the operation.
☐ c. Volunteering to help the Onzigas family was a good thing to do.

Score 4 points for each correct answer.

_____ **Total Score:** Author's Approach

F Summarizing and Paraphrasing

Put an X in the box next to the correct answer.

1. Which summary says all the important things?

☐ a. Dr. Cindy Howard, who worked at the University of Maryland Medical Center, was in Uganda in 2001. She was in visiting a hospital there when a set of conjoined twins was brought in. She found out that the parents were poor. She knew that without help, the twins would die.

☐ b. In 2002 the staff at the University of Maryland hospital did a difficult operation. In an operation that lasted several hours, the doctors separated conjoined twin girls from Uganda.

☐ c. In 2001 conjoined twin girls named Christine and Loice were born in Uganda to poor parents. Without being separated, they would have died. In 2002 a volunteer medical team at the University of Maryland hospital separated them. The girls came through the operation fine and returned home a few months later.

2. Which sentence means the same thing as the following sentence? "None of them wanted a dime."

☐ a. No one wanted any money.

☐ b. Everyone wanted more than just a dime.

☐ c. Not one of them had much money.

Score 4 points for each correct answer.

_____ **Total Score:** Summarizing and Paraphrasing

G Critical Thinking

Put an X in the box next to the correct answer.

1. Choose the statement below that states an opinion.

☐ a. The African names of Christine and Loice Onzigas meant "most beautiful" and "most special."

☐ b. The staff at the University of Maryland hospital did a very kind thing when they separated the Onzigas twins for free.

☐ c. Christine and Loice Onzigas shared a large vein in their hearts.

2. From information in the article, you can predict that

☐ a. the Onzigas family will always remember the medical staff who separated the twins.

☐ b. the doctors at the University of Maryland hospital will do all their operations for free from now on.

☐ c. the next time conjoined twins need to be separated, Dr. Cindy Howard will be able to do it all by herself.

3. Before the operation, Christine and Loice were different because

☐ a. doctors thought they could save only Loice.

☐ b. Christine was growing more quickly than Loice.

☐ c. Loice was growing more quickly than Christine.

4. What is the cause of conjoined twins?

☐ a. Two eggs become joined.

☐ b. There are about 200 conjoined twins born each year.

☐ c. One egg splits just part of the way.

5. In which paragraph did you find the information or details to answer question 4?

☐ a. paragraph 2
☐ b. paragraph 3
☐ c. paragraph 4

Score 4 points for each correct answer.

_____ **Total Score:** Critical Thinking

Enter your score for each activity. Add the scores together. Record your total score on the graph on page 115.

_____ Finding the Main Idea

_____ Recalling Facts

_____ Making Inferences

_____ Using Words

_____ Author's Approach

_____ Summarizing and Paraphrasing

_____ Critical Thinking

_____ **Total Score**

Personal Response

How do you think the doctors felt when they discovered that the twins shared a large vein in their hearts?

_____

_____

Self-Assessment

While reading the article, _____
was the easiest for me.

Compare and Contrast

Pick two stories in Unit Three that tell about how scientists have responded to a problem or a need.
Use information from the stories to fill in this chart.

Title	What problem or need have the scientists looked at?	Which group of people would be happiest if scientists are able to make progress on the problem?	How can people use what scientists have learned?

Which of these ideas do you think scientists should work hardest on? Tell why. _____

_____

_____